The
Christmas
Book

THE CHRISTMAS BOOK

Alice Slaikeu Lawhead

Crossway Books • Westchester, Illinois
A Division of Good News Publishers

Cover design by Ray Cioni, Cioni Artworks.

Illustrations by Jim Carson.

Interior design by Karen L. Mulder.

First printing, 1985

Third printing, 1986

Printed in the United States of America

Library of Congress Catalog Card Number 85-70479

ISBN 0-89107-355-8

To my mother,
Margaret Erickson Slaikeu,
who taught me celebration

Contents

What Is Christmas?

Picture this:

Large, glistening flakes have been softly falling since early this afternoon. The earth is covered with a downy blanket of cotton-candy snow; all is silence and peace on the Northern landscape. It is Christmas Eve, and you have just put the finishing touch on the oyster stew—another dash of white pepper to make it absolutely perfect. The windows of your country kitchen are fogged from the happy baking that has warmed the room. Wiping your hands on the embroidered apron, you hear the sound of sleigh bells in the distance.

You waltz to the bay window in the living room of your colorfully decorated colonial home. Rubbing a pane of glass with the heel of your hand, you see Ray and the children approaching, having returned from delivering the tins of creamy fudge and decorated sugar cookies you make each year for your many dear friends who live in your small New England community.

Opening the heavy wooden door with its magnificent wreath of pine cones and holly, you step briskly onto the porch, invigorated by the frosty snap of the crisp winter evening, enchanted by the scent of burning pine that penetrates the still night air.

As the Clydesdales—Jimmy and Johnny—approach the house, Uncle Fred comes around the side, carrying an armload of wood that he has been chopping. He tumbles it into the old copper washtub that sits on the front porch step and unhitches the horses. The children, eyes shining and cheeks rosy from the ride, scramble out of the sleigh and run to greet you. You wipe their runny noses with the clean hanky in your apron pocket; they don't protest when you do it, of course, because they are full of the joy of the season.

While Ray and Uncle Fred tend to the horses, you lead the children into the house and help them remove their snow pants and coats and mittens and hats. These are hung on the burnished brass coat tree that stands near the ancient potbellied stove, wherein a fire is crackling merrily. The children warm their hands and feet, appreciatively sipping the hot cocoa with marshmallows that you prepared for their arrival and left in an enameled coffeepot on the top of the stove.

While they are toasting fingers and toes, you move through

the living room, charmed by the tinkling of the antique angel chimes. You drink in the combination of smells from the fresh-cut tree and the day's cooking aromas, and begin to hum along with the seasonal music playing softly on the stereo. "All is calm, all is bright . . ."

You now glide into the dining room. The round oak table has a lovely green and red embroidered tablecloth which has been in the family for years. The gold-rimmed china gleams in the candle-light. A repast of roast ham, homemade sausage, sliced cold turkey, Swedish meatballs, oven-browned potatoes, scalloped corn, fresh fruit salad with whipped cream, homemade rye bread, fresh butter from the local creamery, homemade preserves, and of course those jumbo olives that the kids love so graces the board. All that is needed now is the oyster stew and dessert: fourteen different kinds of cookies and confections, all lovingly made from secret family recipes, beautifully arranged on glass platters that sit on the buffet.

The door chimes sound, and you hear laughter permeate the entire house as Grandma and Grandpa come bustling in.

"Merry Christmas, everyone!" they cry cheerily.

"Grandpa! Grandma!" exclaim the children as they race for hugs and kisses in the hallway. Your father has the same old red knapsack slung over his shoulder—the one he brings every year—filled with safe, educational, high-quality toys for the children and thoughtful, tasteful gifts for the adults.

Your mother takes the sack from Grandpa and carefully places each beautifully wrapped package under the balsam pine that you and Ray cut only a few days before, down by the river that runs through the pasture. Your mother exclaims over the fine muslin-and-lace ornaments that grace its even boughs and the small red candles that have been placed on the branches, ready to be lit. But all that will happen later this evening. Right now it's time for Christmas Eve dinner.

You hear Ray and Uncle Fred enter through the back door and chide them with mock-seriousness about tracking in snow all over your clean floor. They return the good-natured banter and boom, "Say, is there anything for two hungry men to eat around here? We're starved!"

"Well, I might be able to find something . . ." you say with a twinkle in your eye.

"I'll just put another log on the fire," says Fred, "and then we'll see what you've got."

"Dinner, everyone!" you call from the kitchen door. You ladle your creamy oyster stew into a big white soup tureen, give a backward glance to the spotless kitchen, and present your Christmas speciality to the assembled loved ones who have seated themselves around the dining room table. There are "Oohs" and "Ahhs" from Ray, Uncle Fred, Mom, Dad, and the children as you position the stew in the center of the table.

"It's beautiful, as always, dear," says Ray. There is enthusiastic agreement on this score, and when all the compliments have been paid, Ray says, "Let's pray." The children bow their angelic heads and fold their clean little hands. The rest of you pass smiles around and wink at each other, happy and content to be together once again in this warm, secure home, because after all—it's Christmas!

———————

Does that sound like Christmas at your house? No? Maybe the next scenario is closer to your experience . . .

———————

"Where are they?" you mutter to yourself as you cram yet another greasy pan into the overcrowded dishwasher. It's approaching 88° F. in your crowded kitchen, and the floor is both gritty and sticky from accumulated sugar spills and the residue of the mustard that crashed onto the linoleum when you opened the overflowing refrigerator this afternoon. "If they don't get back soon, I won't be responsible for this stew . . ."

As you slam the dishwasher closed, you see headlights beam onto the garage and hear a car slosh noisily through the sleet that has been falling since midafternoon. As the car door opens, you hear one of the children scream as if in mortal anguish. Jim yells at them both and comes stomping across the driveway and into the house carrying an armload of plastic Christmas plates filled with broken cookies.

"What are those?"

"Sorry, honey. Half the people weren't there. Should I have left them on the doorstep?"

"If half of them weren't there, what took you so long?"

"Well, the boys weren't very cooperative for one thing. They broke a potpourri jar of Miss Wilkinson's—"

"You're kidding!"

"I wish I was. She was really nice about it, but boy, what a mess! I also had some last-minute shopping to do," he says, and produces a small package from his coat.

"You knew I was waiting for you! I need help to get everything on before your mom and dad get here!"

"Where's Howard? Can't he help?"

"Howard is sitting in front of TV watching boxing and drinking beer. Honestly, if he comes to the table soused . . ."

"I'll go talk to him."

"What about the kids?"

"They can sit out in the car until morning, for all I care. I've had it with the kids."

"Go out and bring them in and give them a cookie or something. Try to get them in a good mood. It's Christmas, for heaven's sake. I don't want it ruined . . ." Your lip starts to quiver.

"All right. But they've had a lot of cookies already. They kept sneaking them out of the plates."

"Oh, forget it. Just get them inside, get them washed up, and then help me with the food. Or work on the fire. It's not doing too well."

"That's because the wood is wet."

"Well, why couldn't we get some dry wood for Christmas? We should have bought some if ours was too green."

"Do you want me to go to the 7-11 and get some?"

"No! Why can't you look at the clock and see what time it is? Your mom and dad are supposed to be here any minute, and we're not even close to being ready!"

"All right, all right! Honey, you've got to relax."

That lip quivers again, and the tears are starting to come too. "When it's over, maybe I'll relax. But right now I'm too busy. I've been on my feet all day, my arches have fallen, my calves are killing me, my lower back has shooting pains, I burned my wrist on the steam from that darn stew, and I've got a headache from eating fudge all day. I haven't had any real food for twenty-four hours."

"Well, I'll get the kids. I think they've quit screaming."

As Jim leaves, you indulge yourself in two minutes of tears before wiping your eyes on the sour-smelling dishtowel that you retrieve from the floor. Just then the front doorbell rings, and your mother- and father-in-law waltz in with a hearty "Merry Christmas, everyone!"

"Hi, Mom, Dad . . . 'Everyone' isn't here. Jim and the kids should be coming in the back soon. Howard's watching TV." Your father-in-law races for the family room, detouring through the kitchen to pick up a beer from the refrigerator.

Your mother-in-law is carrying two shopping bags full of toys. She plops them down by the tree, and the resultant swoosh of air causes a few hundred more needles to fall off the branches.

"That tree's going fast, dear," she remarks helpfully. "Oh, it's so hard to get a decent tree. That's why Dad and I gave up. We like our artificial tree. It's so easy to put up, and it's more economical in the long run. How much did that dried-up old thing cost you?"

"We like cut trees, Mom."

"Well so do I, dear, but my, there's hardly anything left of that one."

"Can I take your coat?"

"Oh, no, I have to get the rest of the presents."

"You give them too much . . ."

"What are grandparents for, dear?" She assumes a mock-serious tone. "It's my sworn duty to spoil those kids rotten. I'll get the rest of the presents," she says as she slips out the front door. You peek into the bag, knowing that they have overextended themselves again on a glut of cheap, sharp-edged toys, half of which run on batteries that they neglected to buy. The gifts that you and Jim picked out so carefully for the boys will look pitiful next to all the shine and glitter.

By the time your mother-in-law returns with her fourth and

final armload of presents, the children have decided to join the rest of the family. They rush to Grandma, begging, "Do you have anything for us, Grandma? Do you have a treat?"

"Well, of course I do, munchkins! Here you go!" She pulls two giant plastic candy canes from her purse and hands them to the boys. They are filled with jawbreaker bubble-gum balls which the children promptly insert into their mouths, competing to see how many they can stuff in at one time.

Your pleas of, "Don't spoil your appetite, we're going to eat soon," are unheeded by the energetic youngsters, who are now all smiles—albeit sugar-induced—and who race up to their bedroom to count the remaining candies.

"So, what can I do to help?" says your mother-in-law as the two of you make your way through a mess of toys and newspapers into the kitchen.

"Not a thing, Mom. Why don't you just go in the living room and relax? I can handle everything just fine."

"Maybe I could wash some of these pots and pans and give you a little more counter space. You know, you really should have a microwave."

"And where would I put that? Really, I don't want a microwave."

"Well, they have these spacesaver models that you hang from your cupboard."

"My cupboards are too low for that. I'd still lose the counter space."

"Oh, I don't think so . . ."

You decide to drop the subject there, highly suspicious that she's bought you a microwave oven for Christmas—a spacesaver model. You don't want a microwave.

You begin to ladle the curdled stew into ceramic bowls from the stove. "Go call the guys and the kids, will you, Mom?" you ask. "Tell them we're eating *right now!*"

You place the bowls at the appropriate places on the table. "That cloth isn't really a Christmas green," you observe as you eye the table critically. "More like chartreuse. I wish I had enough place settings of the good china," you reflect as you place a Melmac plate at your seat. The oyster stew is served, and still no one is at the table.

"It's on!" you shout into the family room. The men there are oblivious to your cry, totally engrossed in a videotape of the eighth round of a regional welterweight amateur bout. Your mother-in-law is now up in the bedroom helping the kids count their jawbreakers.

"Dinner!" you cry once again, but still no takers. You ease yourself stiffly into your chair, untie your soiled apron, and fling it into the kitchen. You survey the dinner of sliced turkey and ham from the deli, brown-and-serve dinner rolls, ambrosia fruit salad, raw vegetables and dip, jello salad, and, of course, cold oyster stew.

Cradling your throbbing head in your chapped hands, you bow your head and pray, "Lord, give me strength to withstand another Christmas . . ."

High Hopes

hristmas for most of us is a collection of fantastic expectations and heartbreaking disappointments. We want a Currier and Ives Christmas and end up with "As the World Turns." And when it is all over, when the tree is back in its box, when the uneaten cookies are beginning to crumble, when the bathroom scale registers seven pounds more than it ever has before, when the front door of the Barbie Dream House is off its hinges, when the Garfield Christmas cards have finally stopped straggling in, when carols are no longer sung at church—we fall exhausted onto the couch and wonder why it wasn't more like what we had in mind.

It used to be different, we reminisce, as we yearn for an old-fashioned celebration. We dream of figgy pudding, handmade gifts, well-behaved children, peace on earth, and goodwill toward men. We long for Christ's presence in the holidays, for a celebration of nativity that takes precedence over all the peripherals of food, decorations, and gifts.

The Way It Used to Be

The first Christmases weren't "Christmas" at all. Ancient cultures whose calendar was based on the sun celebrated the winter solstice in December—a sign that the world would be reborn. The Roman period of Saturnalia was such a time, and is probably the closest ancestor of our Christmas. By the time Christianity became the official religion of Rome, Christ's birth had been elevated to a major holy day, complete with feasting, drinking, dancing, and gaming. In hopes of offering an attractive cultural equivalent to the pagans, Roman Christians observed Christmas concurrently with Saturnalia.

These observances continued in Europe until the Church of England broke away from the Roman Catholic Church. Oliver Cromwell, in the mid-1600s, tried to abolish Christmas altogether as an act of piety and protest against Roman customs. Gradually his influence led to the closing of churches and the opening of businesses on Christmas Day. During this period the Puritans were coming to America, and any celebration of Christmas was also strictly forbidden in the New England colonies as wanton and riotous.

Many people during that time were unwilling to relinquish their most jolly and sacred holiday; so Christmas went underground for a time. Families and friends celebrated secretly in their homes. Eventually it prevailed, helped along by the reign of Charles II in England, a robust monarch who fully supported a hearty celebration. It was reinstated with less revelry than before though, and the Reformation and rise of Protestantism kept it from becoming the orgy it had once been.

The Christmas that *we* are most likely to idealize is not a medieval one, but that of Charles Dickens' *A Christmas Carol*—Mr. Fezziwig, old Scrooge, Bob Cratchit, and Tiny Tim. Dickens' books did a great deal to redefine Christmas as a time for family, friends, and goodwill. This is the Victorian Christmas that is canonized by electronically animated characters in department-store windows, Decorate-A-Tree shops featuring hand-carved wooden or crocheted ornaments, and obscure foods whose recipes are found in the December issues of gourmet food magazines.

Of course, no one *really* wants a Victorian Christmas. Nobody wants to go back to the days when children of seven or eight years of age worked twelve hours a day in underground coal mines or noisy textile factories, when black Africans toiled under slavery in this country, when women literally worked themselves sick tending to home and family, when debtor's prison—not VISA or Master-Card—resolved the discrepancy between income and expenses.

As always, our nostalgia is selective. We want to re-create something that never did exist in reality. We reach for a Christmas that is not merely beyond our grasp, but is not even on the shelf!

Roses are things which Christmas is not a bed of them . . . ,
Ogden Nash

What Isn't Christmas?

Christmas is not a cure-all. Only unhappiness and disappointment can come when we expect Christmas to take care of the problems in the world, the problems in our family, or the problems within ourselves.

Although Christmas sometimes inspires a truce between warring nations, twenty-four hours without firing could hardly be called Peace on Earth. Although Christmas inspires our charitable impulses and prompts us to give money to the Salvation Army or the City Mission or UNICEF, the problems of poverty, injustice, fear, and alienation continue unchecked through the holidays and are often made worse by the season itself.

We want our families to be close and loving at Christmas if at no other time. But as we enter the season, it is clear that our teenage children are still uncouth and bored; Dad is still hopelessly neurotic; our spouse is still battling a losing diet; Grandmother still hates living in a nursing home; and the young children still whine for toys and candy. Rather than solving any of these problems, the glow of Christmas becomes a harsh spotlight whose beams illuminate the fractured family and expose its brokenness and pain.

Beginning the day after Thanksgiving, we set out to create a special sense of Christ's presence in Christmas. We try to meditate on the coming of the Christchild, make a point of listening to religious carols, attend church with greater regularity, send a donation to our favorite charity, and thoughtfully position the crèche on the fireplace mantel. But the staggering number of gifts to be purchased and cookies to be baked, the heavy workload at the office, the Saturday morning pageant rehearsals, and an exhausting holiday party schedule thwart our noble attempts, and we exit the holidays knowing that yet another year went by when we didn't *really* get what we wanted for Christmas.

Christmas will not magically make your apartment large enough to accommodate an eight-foot tree; it will not mystically transform you into a gracious host; it will not make you a good cook; it will not turn you into a patient, creative parent; it will not restore health and well-being; it will not improve your self-esteem; it will not revitalize neglected friendships; it will not pay for itself; it will not heal a broken marriage.

And here's another thing it won't do: it probably won't grace itself with snow either. Over half the people in this country haven't one chance in a thousand of seeing snow on Christmas Day, but are nevertheless disappointed when it doesn't come. Children and adults alike throughout our land look out their windows on Christmas Day and hope to see snow.

Thus, we hope and hope and hope. We don't necessarily do anything about it, but we do hope that somehow, someway Christmas will be different this year. We hope that Christ will settle himself in our hearts as he did in the manger in Bethlehem; we hope our marriage will be restored; we hope our child will come back home; we hope there will be enough money for presents. We hope, we hope, we hope . . .

The trouble, in large part, is that we don't know what our expectations are. They exist somewhere inside of us, unarticulated, and we become aware of them only after they are not met.

On the following page is a list of likely expectations for the Christmas season. Go through this list, considering each statement for a moment or two. Decide if the statement describes something that you want from Christmas. Put an x in Column 1 if it is. In some cases you should specify, if you can, exactly what that statement means to you. Don't worry about whether or not it's a realistic wish. For example, every year I yearn for a nice, festive office party at Christmastime, and my wanting it isn't diminished by the fact that I don't even work in an office. I still want it; so I would put an x in Column 1 beside the statement that mentions office parties.

Take a few minutes to read through the list and record your wishes, adding to the list other desires of which you are aware.

The x'ed statements indicate what you want out of Christmas. If you could have all of them, they would combine to create your fantasy Christmas, perhaps like the one at the beginning of this book. It may be that you want one thing so badly—a family reconciliation, for example—that nothing else matters; maybe you marked only one statement. Or your Christmas wishes may be very complex and varied; it is also possible to have checked nearly every statement, even those that seem to conflict. For example, you might want "more excitement" and "less rushing around" at the same time. And some wishes appear to be incompatible. I marked that I want to keep from gaining weight over the holidays, and at the same time eat, drink, and be merry to my heart's content.

Now you have articulated what you want. The next part of this exercise is to think back on last Christmas (or any typical Christmas), and weigh each statement against that Christmas, asking yourself, "Which of these things *actually* happened? What was it *actually* like at Christmas?" Put an x in Column 2 beside those statements that you can objectively say were part of last Christmas for you.

Do it now.

Christmas generally lives up to your expectations when you were able to x Column 1 and Column 2 for a particular item, or when neither item was checked.

If you indicated that you want to attend church more often during the holidays and enjoy doing so, and if last Christmas you were able to attend more frequently and it was indeed more enjoyable to you than normal, then your goal was reached. Similarly, if you do *not* like to receive extravagant gifts, and the gifts you received last year were definitely on the practical side—just the way you like it—then that nonfantasy was also achieved.

Look back on your list and put a star in front of the statements that represent fulfilled fantasies—that is, statements that have x's in both Columns 1 and 2, or no checks in either column.

Before we move on to the remaining statements—those that flag a gap between expectation and reality for you—I want to say something about Christmas fantasies.

You should not suppose that this exercise is designed to take all the fun out of Christmas, or that its intent is to strip the holidays of the dreams that create magic. It may be the case, for example, that each member of a family whose grown children are scattered around the country will always wish that they could somehow all get together at Christmas. But because of financial restraints, job responsibilities, or any number of reasons, they are unable to realize that fantasy. Still, they hope for something that is highly improbable and nearly impossible. This longing is a special part of their Christmas experience—however melancholy—because it is born out of

The "All I Want for Christmas Is . . ." List

1 2

☐ ☐ To have my immediate family together (spouse, children, and/or parents)

☐ ☐ To be with my extended family (aunts, uncles, cousins, grandparents, nieces, nephews, siblings, etc.)

☐ ☐ Solitude

☐ ☐ Enough money to buy the presents I want to give

☐ ☐ A special spiritual/religious experience

☐ ☐ The kind of celebration I experienced as a child

☐ ☐ Wonderful things to eat and drink

☐ ☐ To be invited to Christmas parties
(specify how many: _____)

☐ ☐ To entertain; to give Christmas parties
(specify how many: _____)

☐ ☐ A substantial Christmas bonus
(specify how much: $_____)

☐ ☐ More involvement with charities and helping the less fortunate

☐ ☐ A nicely decorated home

☐ ☐ To get together with friends

☐ ☐ To receive gifts that are practical and useful

☐ ☐ To receive gifts that are a little extravagant

☐ ☐ Well-behaved, appreciative children

☐ ☐ A truce between myself and family members I don't get along with

☐ ☐ A nice Christmas party at work

☐ ☐ To enjoy seasonal music

☐ ☐ To eat, drink, and be merry

☐ ☐ To attend church more often, and enjoy it more

☐ ☐ Time off work
(specify how long: _____)

☐ ☐ To celebrate my ethnic customs

☐ ☐ To get away: take a trip, go South, go skiing, go on a cruise, do something that gets me away from here
(specify: _____)

1 2

☐ ☐ To celebrate the holidays in our home

☐ ☐ To celebrate the holidays somewhere else
(specify where: _____)

☐ ☐ To go caroling

☐ ☐ A clean house

☐ ☐ To keep from gaining weight

☐ ☐ A break from the traditions I uphold year after year
(specify: _____
_____)

☐ ☐ A change for the better as far as world events are concerned
(specify: _____)

☐ ☐ To hear inspiring music at church

☐ ☐ Opportunity for exercise or physical activity
(specify: _____)

☐ ☐ To see someone special
(specify: _____)

☐ ☐ More excitement

☐ ☐ Less rushing around

☐ ☐ A simpler Christmas

☐ ☐ My family reunited

☐ ☐ To spend plenty of time with my children

☐ ☐ To spend plenty of time with my spouse

☐ ☐ Snow (a white Christmas)

☐ ☐ To go Christmas shopping in a big city where there are beautiful decorations and lots of excitement

☐ ☐ To get all my shopping done early

☐ ☐ To make the gifts I give

☐ ☐ To get lots of Christmas cards from all my friends

☐ ☐ To send beautiful Christmas cards to my friends

☐ ☐ A neighborhood get-together or activity of some kind
(specify: _____)

☐ ☐ To spend less money

☐ ☐ Other wishes:

their love for each other. And who knows? One year circumstances may change, and they *are* reunited. Brothers and sisters who have not been together for years, who have never seen each other's young children, finally get a chance to spend the holidays together—just once—and the yearning of several years is satisfied.

It is not this kind of loving, bittersweet fantasy that worries us. Rather, it is those expectations that foster personal pain, hardship, rejection, frustration, depression, and low self-esteem. These have no redeeming value. They do not make us feel happy or loved or fulfilled; they make us feel like a failure; they cause physical ill-health; they throw a dark shadow over our most meaningful relationships; they threaten our dearest beliefs and values.

Let's think about the scattered family once again. It is, let us say, a young man's dearest hope that his family will be reunited over the holidays. His mother and father are divorced. His mother is remarried and preoccupied with a second family she has started with her new husband; his father is an alcoholic who has never shown much of an interest in his children. This young man's married sister lives two thousand miles away and is raising a large family of her own. His older brother ran away from home when he was in his teens. Our young man was just a boy then and has been out of contact with his brother for over ten years.

When this young man says that he wants to get his family together over the holidays, he is saying, "I want a close, loving family; I want my mom and dad back together; I don't like my mother's husband, and I resent my half-sisters; I wish Dad wasn't a drunk; I wish he loved me; I wish Sis had enough money to fly her whole family here for Christmas; I wish I knew for sure that my brother was safe; I wish I was happily married with a family of my own."

This sort of longing—while completely understandable and legitimate in its proper context—does not have a positive, constructive impact on the young man's holiday celebration. It is very different to long for a family reunion of an emotionally close—though geographically separated—family than it is to desire such a reunion because we believe it could magically change the past or circumstances over which we have no control.

10

Coming to Grips

There are two ways to resolve the tension that exists when expectations are at odds with reality:

1. Revise expectations. In some cases this is a simple task. Having recognized that a discrepancy between expectations and reality exists, you can sit yourself down and say firmly, "Now look here, you must quit getting depressed over the fact that it doesn't snow in Phoenix at Christmas. Think about it for a minute and you'll see that there's nothing to be gained by moaning over the fact that it won't snow this year—or any other year. It would be nice, granted, but it's not in your future as long as you live in Phoenix. You're an adult; this isn't hard to grasp!"

The young man with the scattered family will have a more difficult time of it, since his expectations touch the very heart of major disappointments in his life. He can still revise his expectations, though, by telling himself, "It's not your fault, as you know, but the fact remains that you do come from a broken home, and you cannot change the other people in your family—they are all adults who are living their own lives. It would be nice to have them all together, sure, but there's no point in holding your breath waiting for it to happen. You need to realize that and get on with your life as it really is."

Revising expectations is an option that is available to most of us. To start, you should analyze them with a view to discovering how they came to be part of your fantasies, ferreting out their source.

—How did I get the idea that it was supposed to be like this?
—If I were left to myself, would I come up with this as an expectation?
—If I could have this wish fulfilled, would I be satisfied, or would I just want something different?

Discovering that your unrealistic expectation is the result of a Madison Avenue Christmas advertising blitz, or that you have bought into the super-homemaker image presented in women's magazines, or that your father—a very different man than you—

modeled certain unachievable behaviors will help you put your expectations into perspective.

Some expectations can simply be scaled down. You may wish for a $1,000 bonus from your boss at Christmas; if you get that figure more in line with reality as you know it (based on the experience of past years' bonuses) you can set a more realistic expectation—how about $100? When that happens, $100 becomes a fulfilled dream instead of a booby prize, and anything over that is gravy—a *true* bonus!

The young man we have been discussing might be able to adjust himself to the fact that his entire family will not be together for the holidays, and instead begin to formulate a plan for spending Christmas with his sister and her family, reckoning them to be the nearest thing he has to a happy, loving family.

2. Revise reality. Some realities are not subject to our influence. Few of us are in a position to bring about peace on earth; a single mother on welfare will be unable to buy the gifts she wants to give her children; we can't *make* people send us Christmas cards; the special friend we want to see may be in the Army, stationed overseas; the fact that I don't and won't work in a large corporation rules out the possibilities of a nice, lavish Christmas party with my fellow employees.

When the facts of life are beyond our control, we can say to ourselves: "As much as I want it, there will not be true peace on earth until the Kingdom of God arrives"; "I cannot afford to lavish expensive toys upon my children"; "I do not have the kind of friends who are inclined to send out Christmas cards"; "Since Diana is stationed overseas, I will have to quit thinking about how much I would like to see her"; "If I want a Christmas party, I will have to get a job and work for a big company, and if that isn't an option, forget it!"

This is the best—the only—tack to follow when the reality is beyond our control.

But many realities—more than you might think—are ours to change. Some can be dealt with absolutely and completely. If a white

Christmas is vitally important to you, if you have discretionary funds, and if you live in Arizona and have never been able to reconcile yourself to a cactus Christmas, you can change your reality by driving or flying to Vermont (be sure to check the weather reports before leaving!). It will take a considerable investment of time, energy, and money, but it can be done.

If you are usually disappointed by what you come up with in the way of Christmas greetings, and you do want to send beautiful cards to your friends, you can plan early and carefully to do so. Gorgeous cards can be purchased at half-price after Christmas and saved for the next year; they can be engraved by a stationer; you can enclose a nice snapshot of yourself or your family; you can include a newsy letter inside, one that has been revised and edited by a friend who has a way with words; you can trim the fat from your grocery budget and use the saved money for postage. You can, you can, you can. If you really want to send out lovely cards, or spend Christmas knee-deep in snow, you can.

(Or you may compromise with reality.) While you may be able to find snow in Vermont, the pursuit of a white Christmas could force you to forfeit other important wishes, such as being with family and friends for Christmas, or having enough money to buy the presents you want to give (you spent it all on the plane tickets!). Pursuing one expectation, in other words, could cause disappointment in other areas. Regardless, you have taken the first step toward assuming ownership of your holiday celebration. You have assessed the situation, exercised initiative, and made a choice, aware of the consequences and willing to deal with them.

Sometimes you can get a little piece of your reality. Let's say you want "to spend plenty of time with my children." To begin with, "plenty" is a rather ambiguous measurement of time. But at any rate, you know that you want to spend *more* time with them than you did last year, when they were often left to themselves while you went about your holiday preparations. Part of the problem may be that you are busy at work over the holidays. So early on—in May perhaps—you start planning your work calendar so major projects won't be due in December. In June you ask your supervisor for a week off before Christmas and mentally reserve that time for your kids. As the holidays approach, you do a minimum of time-consuming baking; what you must do is done early and frozen for later use. You decline some adults-only holiday invitations and plan other activities that will include the children (such as a birthday party for Jesus) to which they invite neighborhood friends or schedule family visits to elderly shut-ins from your church. In other words, you revise your reality.

The person who longs for peace on earth can choose to give a special over-and-above money gift to a peacemaking organization; the single mother on welfare could make contact with charitable organizations in her community and let them know she will need help getting Christmas presents for her children; you can begin an aggressive and early Christmas card mailing campaign designed to elicit responses from your friends; you can call Diana, who is in the Army, overseas long-distance on Christmas Eve, even though you won't be able to see her; the young man who wants a family reunion can initiate a yearlong and year-after-year effort to reconcile his family to each other.

My husband and I have resolved that this year the two of us will go to a nice restaurant and have a "company Christmas party," and if we can afford it we will invite some close friends to join us, in appreciation of their support for the work we do.

In revising reality, we say No! to the bombastic advertisements that present unobtainable and nonexistent expectations. We come to grips with the world we live in and take a positive step—albeit small—toward changing what we can. We define our personal sphere of influence and decide to initiate a meaningful dialogue with others who exist within our sphere.

Changing

Revising expectations and revising reality both assume a willingness to change. The rest of this book focuses on some options that are available to us as we attempt to change. Many suggestions are given to improve the quality of your holiday celebration and bring your reality more in line with your expectations. These specifics are presented *not* as yet another thing to be achieved, but as possible alternatives to what is now being done.

In the next chapter, for example, we discuss Advent and its potential for creating a meaningful spiritual experience at Christmastime. If a meaningful spiritual experience is not one of your expectations, or if it is an expectation already fulfilled, then you should not read the chapter on Advent as a blueprint for change that must be followed dutifully.

But neither should you ignore it, since it might strike a chord in you that reminds you that you *do* need something in your celebration that you haven't previously thought important. You can read that chapter—and the rest of this book—with an openness as to how it might benefit you and the people with whom you celebrate Christmas.

The reconciling of expectations and realities often includes other people. Christmas is a gregarious holiday, involving family, friends, store clerks, mail carriers, and society at large. *Everyone* gets into the act at Christmas—from the municipal garbage collector to your old second-grade teacher to your husband's brother's girlfriend. Our personal resolve to make a change or to close the gap may fly in the face of someone we care about or some innocent bystander, and may need some explaining.

By virtue of the fact that you have gotten this far in the book, you are miles ahead of your friends, family, and associates who will celebrate the upcoming Christmas pretty much the way they always have. Therefore, before going off half-cocked about some radical departure, take the necessary steps to lay the proper groundwork for change in those who will likely be affected by your resolve.

1. Broach the subject well ahead of time. Talk with others about your ideas in October, or better still July. If you would like to draw names for a gift exchange between siblings instead of giving a gift to each brother and sister, keep in mind that a well-organized brother may have all his shopping or gift-making done months before Christmas, and could resent your December 15th suggestion wholly on the basis of time and money already expended, although he may be sympathetic to your suggestion conceptually. Allow time for the new idea to sink in and to be implemented.

2. Make sure everyone is feeling good. Do not tack your proposal for change onto the tail end of an argument with your mother, such as "And furthermore, this year I'm going to Florida over Christmas . . ." Instead, pick a time when the concerned parties can discuss the matter quietly, when they are well-rested, well-fed, and in an emotionally receptive state. Avoid discussions that take place when someone has a headache or an appointment to rush off to, when the previous night's sleep has been poor, or when the morning coffee has not yet taken effect.

3. Be upbeat and positive. Give a little background into why you have come up with your idea and why you think it would be a good one. "I have a really great thought for something new and lots of fun we can do at Christmas this year . . ."

4. If possible, avoid making critical statements. It may be possible to implement change without ever telling why you think it is necessary, and this is often desirable. Saying something like, "I think the girls would like—more than anything else—for you to take them to the Museum of Science and Technology this year for their Christmas present," is 100 percent more effective than saying, "They never like those cheap toys you give them—so why don't you just quit wasting your money?" Or, you can suggest a slightly modified Christmas celebration that does not include any alcoholic beverages without accusing Aunt Bea of drinking so much that she is ruining everybody's good time.

When the reason behind your suggestion is crucial for its implementation, by all means share it. Remember, though, that you don't have to change the world overnight. There will undoubtedly be other opportunities to talk to your mother about safe, educational toys for children, and another way to encourage Aunt Bea to face her drinking problem. Little will be gained by making what is supposed to be the lead-up to a happy celebration into an unpleasant showdown.

5. Suggest first those ideas that you think will be readily accepted. If you have a lengthy agenda, address the easy items first. This gets everyone in a good mood and and shows them that different can be better. You might go so far as to include a change that you don't think is especially important or dynamic, but that would create receptivity to some revisions that are more significant. For example, "This year I thought it would be fun if we organized a sledding party for the kids after Christmas dinner," or "Let's just the two of us go out to eat alone one night before Christmas, and then do some shopping together afterward," or "Here's a recipe for peppermint sugar cookies I thought you would like to see."

Once the ground has been broken, and your family or friends see that you have some great ideas, you can approach more significant, and possibly more volatile, changes.

6. Don't try to change everything all at once. A few small changes each year are *plenty*. Even minor adjustments in how you celebrate the holidays can have a major impact on how you feel about Christmas. Removing one thorn in your flesh, Christmas-wise, will give you considerable relief and will create a sense of being in control and aware of what is going on.

If you try to change too much, you may find that you are very unhappy. Something that you have always dreamed of may turn out to be a huge disappointment once accomplished. Although you complain about all the cooking and baking you do, in giving it up altogether you may find that it had a greater meaning to you and was more a part of your ideal Christmas than you ever imagined. Instead of doing *no* baking, try *less* baking for one year. If that feels good, you can keep scaling it down year after year until it's where you want it to be.

Too much change may also make your family and friends unhappy. They may view it as a rejection of them personally, or an insurrection against your relationship. Remember that unless they

17

have been doing some serious and thoughtful evaluating on their own, your suggestions will come like a rock from the sky. As excited as you might be, keep in mind that they are coming at it cold and need some time to adjust.

7. Be open to suggestions and compromise. Be prepared to deal with strong feelings on the part of the people you are approaching. It is entirely possible that they, too, will have things they want to do differently, or that they want some changes you don't agree with. Approach your proposal for change with an open mind; be willing to realign your thinking on the basis of new information that may present itself or shared perspectives you might have missed.

8. Don't be discouraged if your plan fails. You will never know exactly what it's like to change until you give it a try. You may be convinced that you need to have all your shopping done by October, go to great lengths to do exactly that one year, and then come to realize that the bustle and hurry of last-minute gift-buying are an important part of your Christmas magic. You might want to get the family together, but by the 26th of December you know beyond a shadow of a doubt that you never again want that many relatives in your house at once. You may eagerly look forward to having family devotions throughout Advent, but have the entire experience ruined by cynical, uncooperative teenagers.

Don't be discouraged. At least you tried. Take stock of your experiences and learn from them. Next year you'll do *most* of your shopping ahead of time and purposefully leave a few purchases until the 23rd; next year you'll have *some* of the relatives over for Christmas dinner; next year you'll have *personal* devotions during Advent.

Few of us will see our ultimate Christmas fantasy come true. We will never have a big red sleigh pulled by a matched team of Clydesdales, a Victorian celebration in turn-of-the-century London, or cherubic children. But we can, to some extent, bridge the gap between the way it is now and the way we would like it to be. We can refuse to be pushed and shoved and battered by our expectations, and discover how to change our reality.

2

Advent

ne Sunday noon in February I met my friend Lucille for dinner at a buffet restaurant.

"How was the church service today, Lucille?"

"It was terrific! It's Valentine's Day Sunday, you know. The ushers handed out pieces of red paper cut in the shape of hearts, and during the choir anthem we all wrote little love messages and then passed them over to someone else in the congregation."

"Sending Valentines, eh?"

"Right. We'd write things about how much we liked that person, or what they'd meant to us in the past year, or just that we loved them. I got three. One was from the Chairman of the Board of Christian Education, letting me know how much she appreciated my work with the junior highs. Of course, the pastor got the most Valentines of all. Did they do something special at your church for Valentine's Day?"

I'd forgotten all about Valentine's Day Sunday. No, we didn't recognize it in our church. It was the Sunday before Ash Wednesday. The sermon was meant to prepare us for Lent, a call to repentance.

But the church in which I grew up did recognize Valentine's Day Sunday. It began the year. Then there was Easter Sunday. Next we observed Mother's Day Sunday, where recognition was given to the oldest mother, the youngest mother, the mother with the most children present that morning, the mother who came the farthest distance to worship.

Summer was launched with Memorial Day Sunday, followed by Father's Day Sunday, and then Labor Day Sunday at summer's close. That was one of my favorites. Everyone came to the morning service in their work clothes—overalls, lab coat, police uniform, or nurse's outfit.

On Thanksgiving Sunday we thanked God for our many blessings, especially for the pilgrims who settled this country. Christmas Sunday was the climax of the year, celebrating Christ's birth.

And then it was back to Valentine's Day Sunday, and the progression repeated itself.

Those who attend the liturgical churches (Roman Catholic, Lutheran, Episcopal, and others) know that the church has a calendar of its own, that the church year begins with Advent in the first part of December and recognizes dates that have little to do with the holidays mentioned above.

The Christian calendar has evolved over the last thousand years or so, having its origin with Passover, which was probably the first annual observance of the Jews, reminding them how God spared the children of Israel and delivered them out of Egypt. The Jewish calendar is based on a lunar cycle, and that is why Passover (and consequently Easter) falls somewhat irregularly on our Julian (or solar) calendar.

Christmas itself was a concession to the pagan cultures that celebrated Saturnalia or some other winter solstice holiday. Early Christians thought it advisable for the church to provide some major celebration at this time as an alternative to the heathen one. Through the years, certain days were set aside to commemorate the saints (the most familiar to us now is St. Patrick's Day on March 17) and to recognize important milestones in the Christian faith: Epiphany (the twelfth day after Christmas, in commemoration of the legendary arrival of the Wise Men to Nazareth); Advent (the four weeks prior to Christmas); Lent (forty days of prayer and fasting preceding Easter); and Pentecost or Whitsunday (the bestowing of the Holy Spirit after Christ's ascension, and the beginning of the church—seventh Sunday after Easter).

Many of these important holy days and observances degenerated during the Middle Ages into drunken feasts and orgies that were, ironically, sponsored by the Church and intended to commemorate important Christian events. "Fat Tuesday," the day before Ash Wednesday, which inaugurates Lent and a period of fasting prior to Easter, is a good example of a holy day gone wrong. The gluttony of that day (before the lean days ahead) grew into a raucous carnival ("Flesh, farewell!") and can be witnessed during the Mardi Gras celebration in New Orleans, in which hedonistic revelry and drunkenness flourish, obstensibly as a Christian holiday. In recent years devout Catholics have spoken out against the Mardi Gras as an unbefitting prelude to Lent.

John Calvin felt the same way in the 1500s. He observed the lack of piety in the festivals associated with the church calendar, and came to reject the calendar altogether as a blueprint for riotous living and excess. The Puritans who came to this country were very much of that same mind, and they too did not observe the traditional saint's days and commemorative days.

So it continued, on and on, and the rejection of the secularization of church holy days has now turned into the Christianization of secular holidays. Whereas it was once deemed necessary to ban the observance of Lent because of the preholy-day festivities, churches all over the country are now building worship services around such events as Mother's Day, whose roots lie not in the Christian tradition but in the secular.

Many Christians have forfeited the liturgical observances, with their rich tradition, historical significance, and theological relevance, filling the gap with randomly selected holidays that have crept into our culture by virtue of the fact that the business community promotes their existence and encourages celebration via elaborate greeting cards, expensive floral arrangements, and extravagant perfume, lingerie, and other gifts.

It causes one to wonder what meaningless holiday will next be incorporated into the life of the Christian church. Secretary's Day Sunday? Sweetest Day Sunday? Arbor Day Sunday? Grandparent's Day Sunday? In the presence of such attractive festivities, it's a wonder we still celebrate Christmas and Easter! Perhaps this is attributable to the fact that companies like Hallmark and FTD are committed to keeping these two genuine holidays alive for us even though the church is unable or unwilling to take charge of its own destiny where celebrations are concerned.

It would be well for us to return to the church calendar, see what it has to offer us, and consider how its discipline might enrich our own devotional life as it reminds us of the important events in the Christian faith.

Advent and Epiphany

Christmas is bounded on both sides by Advent and Epiphany. Although the commencement date of Advent has varied, it is now generally held to begin on the fourth Sunday before Christmas Day and run until Christmas Eve. It is a period of waiting and of preparation for the birth of the Christchild.

Epiphany marks, symbolically if not literally, the arrival of the Three Kings (Wise Men) at Nazareth to pay homage to Christ. This time celebrates the fact that the Messiah of the Jews also came to redeem the Gentiles, and is Savior of the world.

Certainly it is a very different thing to come to Christmas Day having prepared for it through special Advent services at church, devotions at home, family lighting of the candles in the Advent wreath, the use of a simple Advent calendar, and a four-week focus on the importance of Christ's birth than to wake up Christmas morning with no such preparation, having spent the preceding weeks thinking only of the many gifts to be purchased, cookies to be baked, and decorations to be hung.

Many people have taken up the cry, "Let's not rush Christmas!" and express open dismay at Christmas decorations hung on downtown lampposts well before Thanksgiving, huge displays of Christmas candy at discount department stores even before the Halloween candy has been cleared out, and the incessant Christmas Muzak that blares on shopping mall loudspeakers beginning in mid-November. I, too, share frustration and disgust at such acts, because their sole purpose is to exploit as fully as possible the commercial possibilities of the Christmas season.

But presales and Christmas commercialism have nothing to do with the observance of Advent. Advent is as vital to Christmas as pregnancy is to the birth of a child. During pregnancy, the prospective parents are given time to prepare a place for the newborn in their home and adjust mentally and emotionally to the birth of the child. And the child, of course, is nurtured *in utero* and supplied with the elements necessary to make her a self-sufficient creature who can survive on her own.

During Advent, we are offered an opportunity to prepare a place for the Christchild in our hearts, to adjust mentally, emotionally, and spiritually to his renewed presence in our lives, and to nurture ourselves and those around us so that Christmas does not suddenly appear, but is a long-awaited event for which we are fully prepared.

In the season of Advent, we live out in small part the longing of the world for the Messiah. We experience the yearning of the ages—the yearning for salvation—and enter Christmas with a deep desire for the Christchild to redeem us. We live the symbolism year after year and each time understand more fully our need for him.

Most of us are very impatient; we want what we want, and we want it *now!* The observance of Advent is a spiritual discipline that provides a structure wherein we are encouraged to be patient, encouraged to wait, encouraged to persevere in our hope for Christ's coming.

A strong Advent and Epiphany emphasis can have a very powerful impact on how Christmas is observed. Most of us spend weeks, even months, in preparation for twenty-four hours' worth of celebration. Consequently, it is nearly impossible for the events of that twenty-four-hour period to live up to our expectations. Children are a ready reminder of this apparently inevitable Christmas Day disappointment, sitting amidst a roomful of toys, asking, "Is this all there is?" Without a broader spiritual emphasis, the answer is a regretful, "Yes, that's it. That's Christmas." By observing Advent and Epiphany, we have the opportunity to spread our celebration out a bit, and are freed from the tyranny of doing *everything* on Christmas Day.

Epiphany, or "Twelfth Night," comes on the 6th of January. During those twelve days, we may take time to relax, regroup, enjoy our family and friends, spend time with our children. We celebrate Christ's arrival and reflect on the meaning his birth has on our lives.

We have twelve days to reflect on the importance of Christmas and its ramifications for the coming year. This is a picture of our acceptance of Christ's work and its effect on our personal lives, as well as the larger application of his coming and its implications for all mankind.

The following pages present suggestions for the celebration of Advent. (Epiphany is addressed in Chapter 12.) It is important, once again, to reassure you that the ideas presented here are in no way a "must do" list. Since this book is devoted to reconciling the difference between expectation and reality, bridging the gap between our hopes and dreams and what actually happens, it wouldn't help at all to follow these Advent suggestions as holy writ. Rather, let them stimulate your thinking, break you out of your mold, and open your mind to the possibility of a more meaningful Advent observance as preparation for the coming of the Christchild.

The Crèche, or Nativity Scene

The crèche (literally "crib") is believed to have its origins with St. Francis of Assisi. He was concerned because the people seemed to not truly understand what Christ's birth was like or to fully appreciate the events surrounding his birth in a barn, with animals in attendance; how the shepherds on the hillside were surprised by the angels; how the Three Kings came from far away to pay homage to the Babe.

In 1223 Francis created the first known crèche—a real-life reenactment of Christ's birth—at the church in Greccio, near Assisi, Italy. He included a newborn baby in a manger and Mary and Joseph at first, and in following years added the other participants in the nativity story. People came from nearby villages on Christmas Eve to see the scene, and the popular custom quickly spread throughout Europe.

You may already count a crèche, or nativity scene, as one of your Christmas decorations. In many families, the crèche consists of a small wooden stable, figures of Mary, Joseph, and the Babe in a manger, and perhaps shepherds, assorted animals, angels, and Wise Men. Often the original set has been lovingly extended by the addition of modeled or plaster-of-Paris figurines that children have made in school or at church, and other items have been added: an aluminum-foil star on top of the stable, fiberglass "snow" on which to place the scene, plastic animals from a child's farm set.

Ready-made crèches of all sizes and descriptions are sold during the Christmas season, but they may also be modeled from clay (professional modeling compound or salt-and-flour type), made by painting and firing ceramic greenware, carved from soap or wood, or created by children who employ their own imaginations and materials: Barbie and Ken wrapped in scraps of cloth to resemble Mary and Joseph, Strawberry Shortcake for the Babe, a cardboard box with glued-on hay fashioned to look like a stable, with favorite stuffed animals in attendance.

If we remember St. Francis' concern that the people be able to see graphically what the first nativity was like, then we will look on our own crèche differently. While there are gorgeous, expensive sets to be had, there is also a special meaning when a child's favorite dolls or play figures are used to tell the Christmas story, reminding him that God chose ordinary people and commonplace events to attend the miraculous birth of Christ. The old, chipped plaster figurines from our own childhood, which we faithfully display year after year, underline the rich tradition and meaning of Christmas. Time spent painting greenware, carving figures, or building our own stable provides opportunity for quiet reflection as we create with our own hands symbols that will remind us for years to come of God's wonderful gift.

It has been the custom among some ethnic groups to display the nativity scene with an empty manger, and then to add the Christchild on Christmas Eve. The Wise Men may be placed in a far part of the room and moved closer to the stable each day after the appearance of the Babe until they finally arrive at the stable on Epiphany, the twelfth day after Christmas. Shepherds may similarly be placed at a distance so that they can make their symbolic journey to see the child after he has been born.

Advent Wreaths & Calendars

The custom of lighting the Advent wreath is experiencing a revival in this country. The equipment needed consists of a wreath of some kind on which are placed four candles, one for each Sunday in Advent. The candles may be of any color—red is popular. But traditionally the first three to be lit are pink, the fourth one purple.

The first week, one candle is lit; the second week, the first candle is lit in addition to the second, and so on, until the fourth Sunday, when all the candles are lit (the purple candle is reserved for this last Sunday). Prior to each lighting, an appropriate Scripture passage is read. There is also prayer and perhaps the singing of a Christmas hymn or carol. Some Advent wreaths have a white candle in the center which is lit, along with all the others, on Christmas Eve or Christmas Day.

The lighting of the Advent wreath is a visual reminder that Advent is a time to wait, to reflect on the coming of Christ. Children too young to understand how a calendar correlates with time can often visualize the coming of Christmas with the help of the candles of the Advent wreath.

In the past, our family has made a simple Advent wreath by attaching fresh greens to a circular piece of styrofoam; the candles are lighted after Sunday dinner during Advent. Our simple ceremony consists of Scripture reading and prayer.

Children also love the Advent calendar. These are available in stores that sell greeting cards or can be made at home. They typically show a winter or Christmas scene incorporating twenty-five little doors or windows that are to be opened, one at a time, on each of the twenty-five days of December preceding Christmas. Each little door is numbered, and the child must hunt within the picture to find the appropriate door for each day. When opened, a picture or verse is revealed. The biggest door is #25, which is to be opened on Christmas Day, and often has a picture of the Christchild and Mary and Joseph.

Advent calendars and Advent wreaths provide a daily or weekly reminder that the Christchild will come, that his promised birth will happen, that we must spend the intervening time preparing for the big event.

Devotions

Even those of us who have a difficult time maintaining a consistent devotional discipline throughout the year find ourselves especially motivated to do so during the Christmas season.

Outlines for devotions appear in denominational magazines or Christian periodicals and are often provided by the church. Your minister, pastor, or priest is a good resource for a devotional outline that will coincide with the church's emphasis during the weeks of Advent.

I heartily recommend that every Christian—regardless of denomination or tradition—purchase a copy of *The Book of Common Prayer*, which is the liturgical outline used by the Episcopal churches. The prayer and Scripture readings appropriate to the season of Advent found in *The Book of Common Prayer* are an excellent place to begin when organizing family or personal devotions and observances during the Christmas season. The book contains daily readings, as well as those for the four Sundays of Advent.

The following short book may also get you started on family devotions: *The Gift of Time: Family Celebrations and Activities for Advent*, by Margaret Ehlen-Miller, et al.* It outlines a liturgy for a more Christ-centered celebration, and will be especially useful for families that have grade school and high school-age children who can participate.

Readings

During Advent you can replace your regular reading—newspapers, magazines, romances, technical journals, novels, how-to books, etc.—with seasonal fare. If you spend a certain amount of time each day with your nose in a book anyway, you can—with very little time and effort—prepare for Christmas mentally and spiritually by substituting literature that contributes to your preparation.

Bookstores begin stocking seasonal reading around mid-November. Some books, especially those that are considered classics, can be purchased and made a permanent part of your library. A less expensive way to get books is to check them out from the public library. I recommend the following books and stories for Advent reading. Nearly all of them are available at the library (publishing information can be found in the bibliography).

---

*See bibliography for publishing information.

A Christmas Carol by Charles Dickens. The quintessential Christmas fantasy, the template for our present-day expectations, a moral lesson on charity and loving. The cast: Ebeneezer Scrooge, Bob Cratchit, old Fezziwig, Tiny Tim.

The Best Christmas Pageant Ever by Barbara Robinson. Also a television special, this book tells the story of the Herdmans, the most awful bunch of kids ever, who insinuate themselves into the local church's Christmas pageant and help make it the best ever.

The *Little House* books by Laura Ingalls Wilder. This series of books beautifully describes life on the American frontier. Although any and all of the books would make good Advent reading, the following have specific accounts of Christmas celebrations: *Little House in the Big Woods, On the Banks of Plum Creek, By the Shores of Silver Lake, The Long Winter,* and *Farmer Boy.* Reading about the Ingalls' experiences will help put our modern celebration in perspective.

"The Gift of the Magi" by O. Henry. This short story tells the classic tale of the wife who sold her hair to buy a watch chain for her husband, and of the devoted husband who sold his watch to buy combs for his wife. Included in anthologies of O. Henry's stories.

The Family Christmas Book by Dorothy Wilson. A collection of short stories and cartoons on the subject of Christmas. Warm and soothing reading. Often available at the public library.

Once Upon a Christmas Time by Thyra Ferre Bjorn. The author of *Papa's Wife* gives a reminiscence of Christmas in northern Sweden—the customs, myths, foods, and traditions.

Christmas by William Sansom. A coffee-table book, with color plates and illustrations, that gives a comprehensive history and analysis of Christmas. Beautiful to peruse or study. Well-written prose and beautiful design.

Not all "seasonal" reading is good. For example, I have come to think it's a bad idea for me to spend too much time poring over the

Christmas issues of housekeeping magazines, since they bombard me with advertisements for merchandise that I cannot afford and do not want, recipes for foods I cannot prepare, and patterns for handcrafts I cannot make. I also don't get much out of reading Dylan Thomas' *A Child's Christmas in Wales*, or Truman Capote's *A Christmas Memory*; although highly acclaimed as literature, they don't at all help me capture the mood I personally want at Christmastime.

On the other hand, I wouldn't want to ever celebrate Christmas without having first prepared for it by reading *The Best Christmas Pageant Ever*, which is to my mind one of *the* best Christmas books ever, providing diversion from the drudgery of chores, laughter at my own high expectations, and inspiration about viewing Christmas as though I hadn't the slightest idea of what it was "supposed" to be like.

Christmas reading may be done on your own, of course, but a return to reading aloud as a family might be an old custom you would like to revive—at least for the holidays. Hot chocolate and cookies for parents and children gathered around the dinner table or fireplace make a warm memory to cherish.

Music & Other Media Events

Seasonal music is a big mood-maker for most of us when it comes to capturing the "Christmas spirit." While the piped-in, elevator-variety of instrumental carols and ditties that we hear in department stores, grocery stores, and while on hold when checking your balance at the bank are deemed universally obnoxious and insipid, a band of Sunday School angels singing "Gloria, in Excelsis Deo," or even Bing Crosby crooning his way through "White Christmas" bring back wonderful warm feelings that are an integral part of our Christmas experience.

Since there is no shortage of available music, the challenge is to find the music we like and the music that we can afford.

Many community organizations, schools and universities, and churches provide Christmas programs that are free to the public. These concerts and pageants represent months of rehearsals and years of musical training and are of very high quality. Some are the do-it-yourself variety, as with the recent popularity of community *Messiah* sings where anyone with his or her own copy of the musical score can join voice with hundreds of others who also just want to be a part of singing Handel's *Messiah*.

If you yearn to hear wonderful Christmas music, don't feel confined to what is being offered in your own church or school. Take a chance; see what other groups in your area have to offer. What are some nearby towns planning? Christmas concerts and pageants are advertised in the local paper and on the radio and television.

Recorded music is convenient and involves less expended effort than the concert circuit. Christmas records are available at the library, are sometimes given as promotional items by businesses (the annual Firestone Christmas record album comes to mind) and charities (as a premium for a donation), or can be found in all price ranges at record stores. If you don't have a stereo, tapes can be purchased for use with a cassette recorder—perhaps one that you borrow from a friend for just this purpose.

Local radio stations often take a break from regular programming a day or two before Christmas and broadcast seasonal music entirely. Such programs are often very good. Depending on the format of the station, they will feature the best Christmas music— classical, easy listening, popular, country, or a mixture. Advertising is often kept at a minimum during these special broadcasts, a nice gesture to the season.

My husband and I have lived in several cities in the course of our married life, and one of our dearest Christmas traditions is to tape recorded Christmas music off the local radio station wherever we are, complete with "station identification" and news breaks, and enjoy them year after year. As we hear what the weather was eight Christmases ago when we lived in Chicago, or four years ago in Memphis, we are carried back into a flood of memories of Christmases past.

Many theaters carry holiday movies during the Christmas season. For example, my children enjoyed seeing a Walt Disney version of *A Christmas Carol* one year. Keep your eyes open for possibilities you can see together as a family.

There are many excellent television specials that come around year after year too. Many of them are old movies that have become perennial favorites: *Holiday Inn, It's a Wonderful Life, Miracle on 34th Street, White Christmas.* Others have been made for television and are rebroadcast annually: *Amahl and the Night Visitors, A Charlie Brown Christmas, The Homecoming, How the Grinch Stole Christmas, The Legend of Silent Night, Frosty the Snowman, The Gathering, The Little Drummer Boy, The Littlest Angel, Rudolph the Red-Nosed Reindeer, The Best Christmas Pageant Ever, A Christmas Without Snow.*

Although I would be the last person to advocate an Advent season that revolves around books, records, radio, movies, and television—since these are often passive activities that do not involve family and friends with whom we want to have fellowship—indulged selectively, these media can prepare our hearts and minds for the coming of the Christchild. As disillusioned as many of us have become about the inability of the entertainment industry to incorporate meaningful values into their productions, Christmas is one time of the year when many creative people rise to the occasion and provide wholesome and moral entertainment. If at no other time, the media are worth a second look at Christmas and should be supported for their best efforts.

Assimilating Advent

Now that we have explored Advent, go back to Chapter 1 and your expectations checklist. Pay special attention to the items where expectation is not being met by reality. Could some of these expectations be met through a greater emphasis on Advent? Could you, your family, and your friends benefit by recognizing the time between Thanksgiving Day and Christmas Day as more than four scant weeks in which to do all the baking, cleaning, shopping, and entertaining?

A family in my church celebrates Advent by doing something special each day. One day they bake cookies together, another they go caroling or light an Advent candle, the next exchange a small present, and so on. For them, this is a daily reminder that Christmas is coming; it also helps spread the celebration out a bit, so that everything doesn't happen all at once.

Such an observance in our family would put tremendous pressure on me to be original and meaningful every day; it would further widen the gap between my expectations and my reality. But *you* and *your* family and friends can decide what will work for *you*. A daily celebration might be just the ticket; a more relaxed regimen might be better.

My hope is that this year you will see more possibilities in the celebration of Advent, that you will be open to the idea of waiting and preparing for the Christchild, that you will approach Christmas Day much as an expectant mother approaches her day of delivery— not rushing the event, but prepared, excited, and eager to welcome the child into her life.

Traditions

Because of our traditions, every one of us knows who he is, and what God expects of him.

Tevye, from *Fiddler on the Roof*

hy won't you give a little on this, since you know how important it is to me?"

"What about me? Don't I get any say about how things are run around here? We always do it the way *you've* always done it, the way *your* mother did it, the way *they* did it in the old country."

"That's right. It's our *tradition*. If we don't do it in the same way year after year, it doesn't have any meaning."

"When you do it the same way year after year, it loses any meaning it ever had! All I'm asking is that this year we change just a little bit—"

"There's no such thing as changing a little bit! You change and then everything's spoiled!"

"No one likes that rigamarole. You nearly kill yourself year after year, and for what? Cooking food we hate, putting up decorations that are old and ugly, an aching back from all the hours on your feet, and money down the drain for something no one even likes."

(Sobs) "I can't believe you said that . . ."

"I can't believe you can't believe it! You know it's true. This slavery to tradition is making you and everyone else around here miserable. You try to do everything just the way your mother did, and it's not working. I don't know how she's done it all these years and survived. But even if she enjoys it—which I doubt—it's just misery for you. Give it up, why don't you."

"I can't give it up. It wouldn't be Christmas without—"

"Yes it would! Millions of people have wonderful Christmases without all that junk!"

"Now you're calling it junk!"

And so continues the sometimes silent, sometimes noisy battle with tradition.

A "traditional" Christmas is part of most people's Christmas fantasy. It includes old family recipes handed down year after year, cardboard boxes full of antique ornaments and household decorations that are lovingly unpacked and tenderly placed on the fresh-cut pine tree and around the ancestral home, songs and stories told by the grandmas and grandpas to small children who listen with great eagerness and attention.

The reality for most of us is this: either we have no ancient family traditions to comfort us throughout the season, or we are so busy maintaining the many we do have that we are exhausted and demoralized by our inability to duplicate what our mothers and fathers used to do.

G. K. Chesterton said that "Tradition is merely a democracy of the dead." We suspect that if we fail to do things the way we have always done them, something horrible will happen. Of all the terrible consequences of snubbing custom, the most feared is that "It just won't be Christmas . . ."

Traditions range from the "right" tablecloth for Christmas dinner, appropriate silverware, glass ornaments, and eight inches of snow to a successful batch of peanut brittle from Grandma O'Shea's recipe. And when the old traditions don't work for some reason, it just isn't Christmas.

Sometimes the upholding of tradition is beyond our control: an act of God prevents snow, so we can't go sledding, which we *always* do on Christmas Eve; there was a herring shortage in the North Atlantic this year, and we can't get *sil* at the deli; the state of the family's finances dictates that Mom won't get an expensive piece of jewelry from Dad like she usually does.

Other times, our attempts to uphold tradition are thwarted by other causes: a college-age daughter wants to spend the holidays in Colorado, skiing with her roommate's family; the necessity of overtime hours at work means no Wilton cake in the shape of a Christmas tree this year; Darlene remarried last February and wants to spend Christmas with her new in-laws.

Occasionally an exhausted man or woman will write his or her own Christmas manifesto which states that certain traditions will no longer be observed: cut trees are getting too expensive, so an artificial one is purchased; the family had enough turkey at Thanksgiving, so moo goo gai pan will be served for Christmas dinner; this year, for the first time ever, we will not be going to the farm for Christmas—we're going to have our own celebration at home.

The Good & the Bad

Although we all yearn for meaningful traditions in our lives, we intuitively recognize that while some are good, others are bad—for us.

Traditions, in order to have validity, must be kept because we *choose* to keep them. This doesn't mean that we must each create our own, individually, generation after generation. It means that at some point in our lives we must consciously accept or reject the tradition that has been bequeathed to us, thereby making it our own.

I come from a Swedish family, in which food is central at Christmas. If the food isn't right, it isn't Christmas. My mother went so far as to create a cookbook for our family that specifies which foods are to be included in the family's Christmas Eve smorgasbord, and the recipes for each. It is very specific. There must be one whole, blanched almond in the rice pudding (the recipient of which will, according to tradition, be married in the next year); the rye bread *(limpa)* contains grated orange peel as at no other time during the year; the fruit salad is always served in a cut glass bowl (each child in the family was given one from the family collection, so there would be no slipups).

I decided years ago that I *wanted* to keep the food traditions outlined in that book. I devotedly follow the recipes. There is no substitution of ingredients; nothing is omitted. I would skip celebration altogether before I dared tamper with the Knåkebröd.

That, of course, is my decision to make. There are many of us who are following traditions like this, but we hate it. We never did like *lutfisk*, but each year we prepared the smelly stuff just because that's what one does. We hate jellied veal; it's slimy, but never mind—it's a tradition. We spend days in the kitchen baking hundreds of cookies that will go uneaten (while the Double-Stuff Oreos are instantly devoured), but never mind—it's a tradition. We get up at 5:00 Christmas morning to open gifts when everyone would rather sleep in and eat breakfast first, but it's tradition, and we do it whether we like it or not.

We do all this because we are afraid. We are afraid that if we don't do it, the Christmas gremlins will creep in, ruin our celebration, and spoil everything—and we'll have a rotten time. The miserable time that we have when we observe the lousy tradition is a known quantity. We know the kind of misery that *keeping* traditions causes, and we can deal with it this year because we've dealt with it every other year. But save us from the unknown! Who can imagine what would happen if we quit hanging those ratty old red socks on the mantel! It might spoil everything!

Evaluating Traditions

Although everyone has different traditions they observe or ignore, I would offer the following guidelines for evaluating our traditions.

A good tradition . . .

 . . . is heartily endorsed by each participant. The person who is doing the work, the recipient of the effort, those who are peripherally involved—all think it's great. For example, the bachelor uncle who dresses up like Santa each year, the nieces and nephews whose eyes light up at the sight of him, the parents who provide him with small gifts to give—all must enjoy the charade.

 . . . can be carried out happily, without resentment or anger. The preparation and celebration of the tradition are enjoyable. Although baking involves extra grocery shopping, a sinkful of bowls and beaters, swollen ankles and an aching back, there can still be a profound joy while doing the baking and at the end of a long day spent making the customary goodies.

 . . . accomplishes something worthwhile or necessary. The tradition will often meet a practical need. Charitable giving to a relief organization, in addition to providing great personal satisfaction, is an example of a tradition that is necessary and worthwhile.

 . . . provides a sense of security and continuity. The participants gain a better sense of who they are and where they are going

44

by observing the tradition. Mexican-American children who break a *piñata* are touching base with their ethnic heritage and are assured they can maintain that part of their identity in the future.

A bad tradition . . .

   . . . **is viewed with ambivalence or disdain by one or more participants.** An unappreciative audience is the hallmark of a bad tradition. A family that attends the *Messiah* year after year may drag along three small children who do not appreciate the music, ridicule the soprano, and ruin the performance for their parents and anyone else who sits within twelve rows of them at the concert.

   . . . **is excessively time-, money-, and energy-consuming.** The steep sacrifices required to maintain some traditions can take all the joy out of them. When a person must scrimp and save all year, and give up a needed vacation so he can get time off work and fly across the country to be home for the holidays, he may come to resent the fact that his family requires perfect attendance at Christmastime.

   . . . **is in direct conflict with other traditions.** Marriage, remarriage, blended families, and simple differences of opinion can make a tradition a selfish and meaningless exercise. An insistence by one member of the family that gifts be opened Christmas Eve can spoil Christmas morning for others who have always opened presents the next day; small children in a blended family may be furious at a stepparent who presumes such a change in custom.

   . . . **is based on selective nostalgia.** We remember the past fondly, often forgetting the bad in an effort to recapture the good. The newly-married husband who plans an elaborate celebration "just like when I was a kid" may be forgetting that when he was a kid his mother was abusive, his father distant, and that as an only child he was lonely. His elaborate preparations will fail to re-create his happy childhood for the simple reason that it never existed.

   . . . **manipulates its participants.** Adherence to custom can mutate into an unwillingness to let oneself and others grow. The parent who insists that grown children participate in some ill-conceived traditional celebration may be using that custom to trick his/her children into returning home and being dependent upon him/her once again, thereby stifling their natural maturing process.

The following chart will help you evaluate the traditions you are following or considering. For the purposes of this exercise, traditions have been divided into three categories:

Old Family Traditions are those that have been around longer than you. Examples might be ethnic household decorations, opening presents on Christmas morning, going to church on Christmas Eve—if they were started by someone other than yourself a long time ago and you are still observing them.

Present-day Traditions are those you have instituted. The sending of a Christmas letter every year, charitable giving during the holidays, decorating your tree with strung popcorn and cranberries are all examples of possible present-day traditions.

New Traditions were part of your celebration last year, and maybe the year before, but are not yet firmly established. They might include attending the office Christmas party, or trying out a new caramel corn recipe given to you by a friend, or a custom you inherited through a recent marriage.

Take a few moments to chart some traditions that you are following in each of the three categories.

A tradition must have some discernible value if its observance is to be justified. For some people the value may lie simply in the fact that it *is* a tradition—that's enough. Most of us, though, demand some other virtue than We've Always Done It This Way.

Return to your chart. Mark an x in the Values column for each statement that accurately describes your tradition. If you are unsure, mark it with a ?; if the criterion doesn't apply, leave it blank. There is a space for you to give credit for a tradition on the basis of some other personal value that isn't mentioned. At the bottom of the page, describe its value. Be specific. When you are done, add up the x's in each row and you will arrive at a point value (0-7) for each tradition. Do this now, before proceeding.

Each tradition now has a point value attached to it. As you look at your own evaluation of the traditions you follow, you may see that the ones with high point values are the ones that you want to maintain the most; those with low point values are not particularly important to you.

However, it is possible for a low-point tradition to have tremendous significance. For example, I got a low-point value for shopping for toys. I don't like to do it much, it gives me no security, my friends couldn't care less that I do it, and it isn't necessarily worthwhile; *but* my family appreciates it (particularly my children, who are the recipients), and it is necessary in a sense. Therefore, I don't intend to quit shopping for toys at Christmas.

The point values will, by and large, confirm what we already know or feel about our traditions. Those that we wouldn't think of changing generally get high marks on this chart. But traditions that do not coincide with our values are traditions that should be scrutinized and possibly changed. The assigned point value gives us permission to entertain the possibility of either continuing or abandoning a particular tradition.

Change, as we have said earlier, is often difficult, since *you* must change (that's hard enough) and invariably others must change too. For example: even—make that especially—if *you* are ready to give up your traditional extravagance when it comes to buying gifts for the rest of the family, *they* may not be willing to forego that tradition. Even if you wish to let someone else direct the church Christmas play this year, the fact that no other capable and willing person can be found to do it in your stead may mean that you will do it anyway.

New Becomes Old

So much for unencumbering ourselves of burdensome traditions. What about those of us who need some traditions?

A young couple, newly married, may be looking for traditions that they can begin celebrating together. Each will undoubtedly bring some of their own to the marriage, but they will also want to arrive at some observances that recognize their relationship. Very often the establishment of a new, joint tradition is an answer to the question of how old, conflicting traditions will be resolved. *He* always had turkey for Christmas dinner; *she* always had ham; *they* settle on roast duck.

Others are curious about their "roots." They have a strong

The
Tradition
Checklist

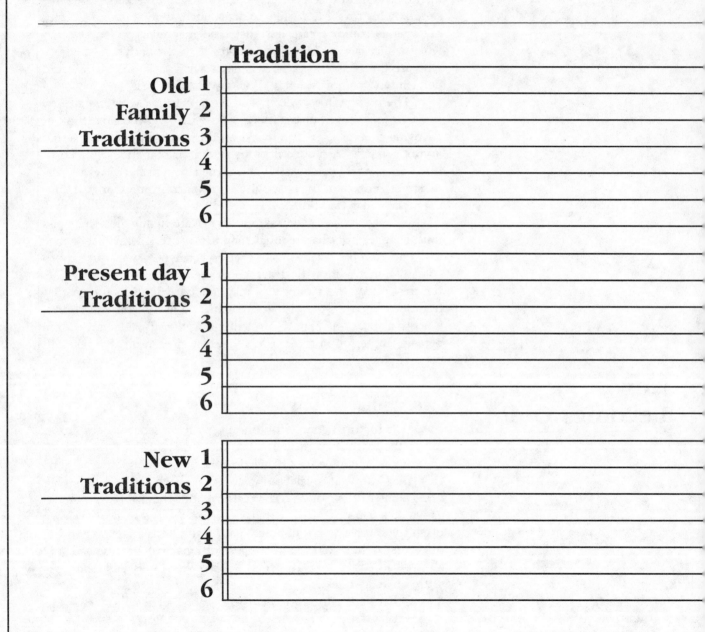

Tradition

Old
Family
Traditions

1
2
3
4
5
6

Present day
Traditions

1
2
3
4
5
6

New
Traditions

1
2
3
4
5
6

I LIKE IT	MY FAMILY APPRECIATES IT	MY FRIENDS APPRECIATE IT	IT GIVES ME SECURITY	IT ACCOMPLISHES SOMETHING WORTHWHILE	IT IS NECESSARY	OTHER VALUE*	TOTAL (# of "x"s' IN A ROW)

* SPECIFY:

interest in their ethnic heritage, in their family background, in customs of the past. Many times these people come from families without meaningful traditions, and their desire to revive the old arises from a deep need for security and stability.

For whatever reason, if you are looking for traditions here are some places where they can be found:

1. Think back on past Christmases, especially those of your child-hood. Can you remember something that you used to do that you would like to start doing again? What was most pleasant? Do that. What did you hate? Forget it. Keep in mind that memories can be deceiving. Before determining to duplicate your bygone holiday, reflect as objectively as you can, being as honest with yourself as you are able, and evaluate the events of your childhood Christmas. Was it such a happy time for you and for the others around you? Are you being realistic about your ability to re-create it? Will your family and friends support you in your quest?

2. Interview other family members about family traditions. Talk to your sisters and brothers, your parents, grandparents, aunts and uncles and cousins. Can they give you some leads about family traditions? There may be wonderful old customs which your branch of the family tree abandoned for one reason or another that could be happily recovered.

3. Go to the library and research ethnic customs. There are scores of books dealing with Christmas (and other holiday) customs around the world. Concentrate on the traditions of your ethnic background. If you have no traceable heritage, or come from a country without Christian traditions, look to the part of the United States in which you now live or that your family is from. The South, Pacific Northwest, New England states, Great Plains—every part of this country celebrates the holidays in its own unique way.

4. Work from your own fantasies. Think about your ideal Christmas. After you have discarded the unobtainable magic (little elves that do the dishes while you are sleeping, a mysterious check for

$1,000,000 that arrives in the Christmas Eve mail, etc.), pick out some ideas that you can incorporate into your celebration. It may have nothing to do with your own past or your ethnic heritage, but if you think Christmas could be improved by implementing part of your fantasy, that's reason enough to try a new custom this year.

5. Ask friends to share their traditions with you. Better yet, ask them to include you in their celebration. It's great fun to cooperate on holiday baking, plan a reception together, or have a tree-trimming party. Since many traditional activities involve an extra dose of time, effort, and money, you may find that your friends are excited at the prospect of your participation. There are some traditional activities that are very intimate, and you won't want to crash someone else's celebration in such a case. On the whole, though, you can form a very satisfying partnership with a friend who has something to share in terms of tradition—if you have something to share in terms of help.

6. Peruse homemaking and women's magazines. Magazines such as *Better Homes and Gardens, Redbook, Family Circle, New Shelter, Parents Magazine, House and Garden* are filled with ideas for holiday celebrations. You can see in glossy four-color what a certain dish looks like when properly made or how a tree looks when it's trimmed with homemade ornaments of a certain type, or get patterns and directions for Christmas crafts and ideas for family activities. These helps are also available in books you can find at the library. Be careful, though. Many of the suggestions that appear so fabulous in the magazine or book are nigh on impossible to re-create on your own. If something looks too difficult to do—well, it probably is. Still, you can get some wonderful ideas to be used year after year—beginning a tradition.

Commitment to The Way We've Always Done It can be a continuing pleasure or a tremendous burden.

Times change, people change. Growing children, personal development, the addition of new family members (some of whom arrive with their own traditions), and a changing society make traditions at the same time more important than ever and less meaningful than before.

The parent who is afraid to adapt to life without children at home will panic when a married daughter announces that this year their new family will not be coming to Grandma's for the holiday, or may become severely depressed when a college-age son decides to travel over Christmas in abandonment of the family celebration.

"But we always get together! It just won't be Christmas without you!" cries the distressed parent. "Please come home! I'll miss you so . . ." These pleas create guilt for both parent and child, and make tradition the scapegoat for a family that is growing up and, perhaps, growing apart.

Children caught in the bind decide that tradition is crummy. This is a tragedy of the sixties: that millions of young people, searching for identity, rejected that aspect of their existence which held so many answers—family and cultural traditions—in their quest for themselves.

The pendulum has swung. We are now apt to latch on to anything that connects us with our past, whether it has intrinsic value or not. We have given up control over our lives. We're tired. We want some security, some stability; so we reach for the old with little regard for its merit.

When traditions, and traditional celebrations, are fun to do, fulfilling for all participants, and give a genuine sense of security, they will perpetuate themselves. Although they may be modified from one year to the next, their spirit will survive, because no one will want to give them up. The best traditions will, as Tevye says, tell each one of us "who he is, and what God expects of him."

Logistics

ete, a bachelor systems analyst, has decided that he will be making some changes in the way he celebrates Christmas. He's going to have daily devotions during Advent, using *The Book of Common Prayer* as his outline. He's decided to give a special over-and-above gift to World Vision and is going to make an effort to bake some of his own Christmas cookies this year instead of relying on the grocery store bakery. He believes that these few modifications in his celebration will help him have a holiday that reflects his values more than it has in past years. In order to accomplish his goal, he will need to practice personal discipline.

Elaine, a divorced mother of three, has also decided to make some changes this year. She wants to help her children become less "gimme" oriented, and work on some ways that they can learn to give and share with others. She would like her ex-husband, who is remarried, to agree to let the children stay with her over Christmas this year (although they are supposed to be with him, as stipulated in their shared-custody agreement). Part of her strategy with her kids involves spending extra time with them making (instead of buying) gifts, visiting elderly residents of a nearby nursing home, and doing volunteer work at the county hospital. However, with her responsibilities as assistant principal at the public high school, she will be very busy with work up until December 22. The changes that she wants to make will involve the cooperation of her three children, her ex-husband and his wife, and her co-workers at school—as well as a megadose of inner determination.

It's one thing to resolve to have a more value-centered celebration, and yet another to make it a reality. The single person like Peter, who can act pretty much on his own, is in a different situation than someone like Elaine, whose life is wrapped up with others whose behavior and attitudes affect her own ability to make a change.

A Plan

Change takes a plan; it needs a strategy.

By now, you probably have some definite ideas about changes

you want to incorporate into this year's celebration. You've thought of something that you want to do differently, something you have never done before that you want to begin, something that you've never been happy with that you are ready to abandon.

But if you don't have a plan, if you don't have a strategy, the inertia caused by years of business-as-usual will prevent you from realizing your dream. Even if your Christmas fantasy contains a great deal of spontaneity and spur-of-the-moment fun, you must have a plan. Lacking a clear-cut scheme and the organizational tools with which to carry it out, you will slip back into what you've always done, or what is easiest, or what is expected of you, or what you know how to do. And when Christmas is over, you'll wonder why you ever thought it could be any different than it has always been.

Most of us will need to start with "family planning." Every member of your family who will be affected by the change must plan with you. This includes spouse, children (even preschoolers), parents, in-laws, everybody.

Ideally you will be able to hold a famiy council with those members of your family who live with you or close by. Those who are far away will need to be communicated with some other way. A letter would work, but a phone call is better since there is give-and-take in negotiating the celebration.

The meeting should take place well before Christmas. October or early November would be great. (Maybe it's already too late to do that. If you're reading this on the 21st of December, you can still have a meeting and arrange some parts of your celebration together.)

SUMMONING THE TROOPS

Do *not* broadcast your intentions like this: "Tonight at 2000 hours sharp we will convene in the kitchen, at which time I will explain to you cretins what you are going to do to make my Christmas this year less miserable than the last."

Try another approach, such as, "Thursday evening, after supper, we're going to stick around after we're done eating and talk about our Christmas celebration."

SWEETENING THE DEAL

". . . And there will be homemade donuts," you add to the invitation. You might present the meeting as a cookie party, or make popcorn and have soft drinks, or fix hot chocolate. Food always helps, if for no other reason than that people will want to come. Make sure that all participants are relaxed and fed before proceeding.

OPENING EXERCISES

Begin by giving everyone a blank sheet of paper on which you have written the following starter sentences:

"What I like most about Christmas is . . ."

"What I like least about Christmas is . . ."

Allow a few minutes for each family member to complete the sentences (with more than one thought for each, if necessary). Preschoolers can express themselves verbally, if they like. Let children speak their mind without any interference or censoring at this point. If your youngster says, "The thing I like most is getting lots of presents," let that statement stand. He's entitled to his opinion. You should not use this opportunity to explain that Christmas is more than getting presents, that since Dad's out of a job there won't be presents this year, or that it's time he started thinking about whether he's been naughty or nice.

THE MEAT OF THE MATTER

Give family members a chance to share their sentences, without comment from others. When everyone has shared, including you, direct a discussion of how this year's celebration could encompass more of the qualities family members like best and fewer of those that are liked least.

Your discussion may uncover several changes that could be made. It is probably best to make only one or two per year. These can be determined by acclamation or majority vote.

BRASS TACKS

Once you have decided what will happen, then you need to figure out who is going to make it happen.

Give family members an opportunity to volunteer for certain responsibilities, especially those that relate to their own preferences. For example, if Granddad wants a real tree this year instead of the artificial one, then he should be in charge of tree hunting. If Donny wants to have a birthday party for Jesus, let him compile the guest list, work on the invitations, and make decorations. If Mom wants to go shopping in the city this year, let her research train schedules, places to eat lunch, and stores that she wants to go to. If you want more opportunities to be with the kids, no one but you can arrange to get the necessary time off work.

These responsibilities can be written down, and it's a good idea to put a completion date along with them: the tree must be up by Thursday, the invitations out by the 14th, the shopping trip planned by Saturday, and you must talk to your boss tomorrow.

DUTIES OF THE MODERATOR

Since this meeting was your idea (Okay, it was my idea . . .), it is your role to minimize controversy and encourage open discussion and exchange.

When one Christmas custom shows up on your mother's "I like it best" list, but is definitely your least favorite thing, there may be hurt feelings or expressed anger. Take it on yourself to be the voice of encouragement, the reconciler. Even if there isn't unanimous agreement on a change you really wanted to make, you will have gained something just by virtue of the fact that it was discussed. Next year it might actually change. Be willing to let your own desires take a back seat to those of others, especially at the start of the discussion. Once other family members see that their own opinions are being encouraged and respected, they will be more open to hearing and acting on yours.

So here is your agenda for the family meeting:

1. Set the meeting at a convenient time.
2. Provide refreshments.
3. Explain the purpose of the meeting.
4. Pass out sheets of paper with, "What I like most about Christmas is . . . ," "What I like least about Christmas is . . ."

5. Share completed sentences.

6. Discuss possible changes and modifications in the celebration.

7. Volunteer for or assign responsibilities to implement change.

8. Record responsibilities and date by which they will be done.

9. Adjourn, with thanks to all participants.

If important family members are unable to attend the meeting, you can write a letter explaining what you want to accomplish, and ask them to complete the two sentences. Then either by mail or over the phone you can share your completed sentences and discuss the changes that might be made.

Structure your meeting as you see fit. Just make sure that it's as positive as you can make it.

Personal Planning

Now that you have come to some sort of consensus with your family, you are ready to concentrate on what *you* will be doing. If your celebration doesn't involve a cast of thousands (if you're like Pete, in other words), this is where you start figuring things out.

Your personal planning will center around time and money. We'll start with time.

It is, of course, an immutable law of nature that if two worthwhile events take place in a year's time, they will always happen on the same day. Nowhere is this fact more evident than during the Christmas season.

The office party and the school pageant are the same Friday afternoon; your college roommate (whom you have not seen for thirteen years) will be in town on Thursday night, which is also the night that you are performing with the Civic Symphony; your company's busiest season of the year is right before Christmas, when things are also busiest at home.

Some conflicts are unavoidable; others are our own doing. We could pick any of a dozen nights to trim the tree, but put it off so long that we absolutely must get it done before the cookie exchange tomorrow, thereby having to miss attending the final performance of the Christmas cantata at church (they've performed it four times, but you missed all those because . . .). When poor planning, procrastination, or lack of communication are the cause of conflicts, missed opportunities, and last-minute panic, there is a solution.

A special Christmas planning calendar, faithfully maintained, is your best hope. This is different from the calendar that hangs in your kitchen or sits on your desk, although it may contain much of the same information. It is a two-month calendar (November and December) on which you can record your Christmas schedule and opportunities (see sample).

First, record all those activities and events that are non-negotiable, those over which you have no control. These include important functions to which you have been invited, church and community programs, Christmas itself (much as you'd like to, you can't change *that* date), arrival times of visiting relatives and friends, and other "givens." Mark them in ink to signify that they are unchangeable.

Now get your pencil out and note your own planned activities: holiday entertaining, departure time for trips, time off work, etc. As much as possible, space those with respect to the activities already on the calendar. For example, don't have your daughter's slumber party the same night that Rick and Sylvia arrive from Kansas City. That's a conflict, and you do *not* want a conflict. Some events can be arranged that you might not think are very fluid. Even a birthday celebration can be moved up a week or two or postponed a few days if it won't get the proper attention it deserves without that adjustment. Very young children (who aren't into calendars) and adaptable adults may be more than willing to celebrate a holiday-season birthday at some other time when it won't get lost in the shuffle.

Note preparation time: baking days, days for housecleaning, decorating, setting up the tree, making gifts, shopping, wrapping, and delivering gifts. Include such deadlines as the date by which you want to have your Christmas cards and packages mailed (especially overseas mail), the shelf-life of baked goods, the availability of friends and family to help with preparation, time needed to complete craft projects, and so on. Remember that your energy is limited

November Schedule

Sunday	Monday	Tuesday	Wednesday	Thursday	Friday	Saturday
	1	2 Overseas Packages Mailed TODAY	3	4	5	6
7	8	9	10	11	12	13
14	15 Christmas Letters to PRINTER	16	17 Wilkinsons for dinner	18 ALL HOMEMADE GIFTS done by TODAY!	19 PICK-UP christmas Letters from PRINTER	20 10:00 Christmas Pageant Rehearsal
21	22	23	24 WORK ON CHRISTMAS LETTERS!	25 Thanksgiving	26	27 10:00 Christmas Pageant Rehearsal
28	29	30				

December Schedule

Sunday	Monday	Tuesday	Wednesday	Thursday	Friday	Saturday
			1 7:00 Advent Service	**2** Shopping with DICK (off work)	**3**	**4** 10:00 Christmas Pageant Rehearsal COSTUMES!!
5 CHRISTMAS PAGEANT 7:00 Bring cookies	**6**	**7** MAIL Christmas Letters	**8** 7:00 Advent Service	**9** Joan's school program 2:00	**10**	**11** 9:00 Bible Study Brunch (ALMOND COFFEE CAKE) at Harris' house
12	**13** Kids at Mom's 10:00-2:00 Baking	**14** Baking	**15** 7:00 Advent Service	**16** Baking	**17** Allied Christmas Party 7:00	**18** CLEAN CLEAN CLEAN! S.S. Class caroling party 8:00
19 3:00 The Messiah CIVIC AUDITORIUM	**20** Mom & Dad arrive 7:56 PAN AM 858	**21** Last Day of School!	**22** 9:00-2:00 Janet's kids here 7:00 Advent Service	**23** 9:00-2:00 Kids at Janet's	**24** 11:00 P.M. Candlelight Service	**25** CHRISTMAS
26	**27**	**28** 3:30 Birthday Party for Jesus	**29**	**30**	**31** 9:00 Reception at Mudgua's 10:30 Watchnight Service	

and that too much going on at any one time will ruin you and will ruin your holiday.

It is at this point that you may see the sense in doing Christmas baking in November and freezing it; keeping the two days before Christmas absolutely clear of responsibilities so you can handle the inevitable last-minute details; having your New Year's Day brunch on Valentine's Day this year.

As you work with your calendar, take into consideration the calendars of family and close friends with whom you will be sharing your celebration.

Calendar events are not chiseled in limestone; they can be added, dropped, and rearranged as needed. As the season progresses, you will get new information and may want to exercise flexibility in your planning. A Christmas planning calendar—faithfully maintained and constantly consulted—will help you evaluate your responsibilities and minimize conflicts and disappointments.

Financial Planning

"I wish I had had the money to give him the nicer billfold. There was a beautiful calfskin tri-fold that he would have liked, but by the time I got around to shopping for him, I only had enough left for one of those nylon sports wallets with the Velcro closure . . ."

"I know I overspent again this year, but it's impossible to keep within the budget. I can tell you I don't want to be around in January when the credit card statements come in—we just got last year paid off!"

"Sure it cost me an arm and a leg, but it's what she wanted, so I got it for her. I'm no cheapskate!"

"We made a lot of gifts this year, but they ended up costing more than if we'd bought presents. I suppose they were more appreciated, but . . ."

"There won't be any Christmas this year. We don't have any money. I don't know how to break it to the kids."

Lack of financial planning—and lack of finances—are blamed for many holiday disappointments.

Although we may contend that Christmas is more than presents—and it surely is—the fact remains that it takes money to produce the celebration we want.

Everything costs. Even freebies, like a company Christmas party, require money for the baby-sitter, money for parking, money for a new dress or suit or tuxedo rental, money for the gift exchange, money to go out with friends afterwards, money, money, money. Simple homemade gifts require money for craft materials, and the most economical holiday recipes still call for special (expensive) ingredients.

Some people seem to always be able to come up with the money they need. They get a Christmas bonus every year to pull up the slack, or join the Christmas Club at the bank, faithfully depositing throughout the year so they can have the money they need to celebrate the holidays in the manner in which they have become accustomed. My mother-in-law does Christmas shopping all year 'round in order to minimize the end-of-the-year crunch, and socks away twenty-dollar bills in her freezer ("cold cash") beginning in August, so that the holidays are fully funded by the time they arrive.

Others of us (I think we're in the majority) enter the Christmas season with our finances in the same disarray that exists during the rest of the year. By December 12, our modest savings are depleted, the bank is sending threatening letters about the checking account, and half the gifts and most of the decorations are yet to be bought. We enter the Checking Plus stage by the 19th. When the 24th comes around, it is clear that the credit cards have been through a terrible ordeal—they are cracked, nicked, and split from continuous heavy use.

In January, the bomb drops. Your husband assumes his role as Dagwood Bumstead by waving a handful of charge slips and bank statements in front of your face, exclaiming: "Look at me; do I look like the Denver Mint to you?" And you, the charge-happy wife (a la Blondie), lament, "Okay, next year *you* can do all the shopping and baking and wrapping and mailing and boohoo, boohoo, boohoo . . ."

So it goes. The battle is played out between husband and wife, parent and child, or self vs. self. It is the money problem that brings many people to wish for a simpler Christmas of bygone years, without admitting that those Christmases, too, were a strain on the family finances.

A budget is what is needed. And not just a simple, "Let's see, I've got thirteen people to shop for, at $10 a gift. That'll be $130 and extra for groceries and the tree. I think $200 will do it."

No, you're going to have to be more detailed, more specific. You're going to have to look for all the hidden costs, remembering that prices go up from one year to the next, and making provisions for last-minute expenditures. You're going to have to spend more than three minutes working it all out.

The following pages contain a budget outline that covers virtually every extra expense that you will encounter during the Christmas season. At this point you may have resolved to have a simple Christmas, to quit exchanging gifts between family members, not to take the trip to Aunt Sue's, to forego all entertaining. But don't be fooled into believing that Christmas won't cost this year, because it definitely will. Unless you are going to ignore the season entirely, and have enlisted the cooperation of every friend and relative in that resolve, it will cost. And if the changes you are planning are of an inclusive nature—that is, you will be doing additional activities this year—then you must count the cost.

Go through the budget now, and estimate as best you can what you will realistically be spending for every applicable item. If you are in doubt as to how much something is going to cost, figure it high. Write your estimated amount in Column A. Do your budget now—in pencil.

Your grand total for all Christmas expenses is undoubtedly staggering, and—this is the worst part—it is undoubtedly accurate. You can see now why January and February are such killer months. Even though you planned for the obvious expenses in previous years—gifts, entertaining, and such—the extra hot water that your

The Christmas Budget

	A	B
CHRISTMAS GREETINGS	$	$
Commercially made cards		
Photo inserts (film, processing, prints)		
Printing of Christmas letter		
Envelopes		
Manufacture of homemade cards		
Seals, stickers		
Long-distance phone calls		
Telegrams, mailgrams, etc.		
TOTAL GREETINGS	$_____	$_____

	A	B
POSTAGE AND FREIGHT		
Packages to be sent		
No. of pkgs. _____ x $ .00/pkg.		
Christmas cards		
No. of cards _____ x $. /card		
(domestic)		
No. of cards _____ x $. /card		
(overseas)		
Other holiday correspondence		
No. of pieces _____ x $. /piece		
Overnight or Express-Mail service		
No. of pieces _____ x $ /piece		
TOTAL POSTAGE	$_____	$_____

	A	B
GIFT WRAPPING		
Wrapping supplies		
Boxes		
Paper		
Bows		
Tags		
Tape		
Novelty attachments		
Professional gift-wrapping		
No. of gifts _____ x $2.50/gift		
Kraft paper, tubes, boxes, twine, labels, tape for wrapping pkgs. to be sent		
TOTAL WRAPPING	$_____	$_____

	A	B
GIFTS (record name of recipient and cost of buying or making gift)	$	$
Family Members		
1		
2		
3		
4		
5		
6		
7		
8		
Friends		
1		
2		
3		
4		
5		
6		
7		
8		
Charities and/or organizations		
1		
2		
3		
4		
Employees and/or co-workers		
1		
2		
3		
4		
Service people (newspaper carrier, mail carrier, doorman, etc.)		
1		
2		
3		
Other		
1		
2		
3		
TOTAL GIFTS	$_____	$_____

	A	B
FOOD AND SERVING	$	$
...king ingredients (especially needed for cookies, cakes, etc.)		
...li items (meat, cheese, prepared foods)		
...aples		
...Monthly food budget ($_____ ÷ 2)		
...tchen paraphernalia (cookie sheets, pans, decorating tools, etc.)		
...tchen and table linens		
...per plates and cups		
...eals eaten in restaurants		
No. of meals _____ x $_____/meal		
TOTAL FOOD	$_____	$_____

...ECORATING
- ...hristmas tree and stand
- ...hristmas tree decorations
- ...ousehold decorations
- ...reenery (wreaths, garland)
- ...andles
- ...esh and/or artificial flowers
- ...utdoor decorations
- ...utdoor lighting
- ...ther:

	A	B
TOTAL DECORATING	$_____	$_____

...ICTURES
- ...ilm: _____ rolls at $_____/roll
- ...eveloping: _____ rolls at $_____/roll

	A	B
TOTAL PHOTO	$_____	$_____

...CLOTHES (for each family member, list what will be needed and estimated cost)

	A	B
TOTAL CLOTHES	$_____	$_____

	A	B
TRAVEL	$	$
Gasoline for errands, around-town trips		
Bus, train, subway fares for errands		
Long-distance travel		
1. Mileage or airfare		
2. Meals on the road		
3. Lodging		
4. Miscellaneous		
TOTAL TRAVEL	$_____	$_____

ENTERTAINMENT
Entertaining others:
- Function: _____
  - Food cost
  - Beverage cost
  - Invitations and postage
  - Miscellaneous
- Function: _____
  - Food cost
  - Beverage cost
  - Invitations and postage
  - Miscellaneous

Being entertained:
- Formal clothing rental
- Hostess gifts

Baby-sitting
- No. of days/nights ___ x $_____/night

New clothes (if not included in Clothes budget)

	A	B
TOTAL ENTERTAINMENT	$_____	$_____

MISCELLANEOUS
- Seasonal albums and tapes
- Movie, play, and concert admissions
- Professional housecleaning
- Professional carpet cleaning
- Professional yard work
- Costume rental (Santa Claus suit, etc.)
- Redecorating: Interior
- Redecorating: Exterior
- Utilities (estimated overage for overnight guests)
- Other:

	A	B
TOTAL MISCELLANEOUS	$_____	$_____
GRAND TOTAL	$_____	$_____

brother and his family used during their two-week stay, the mileage put on your VW as you ran innumerable errands, and the meals eaten at Arby's because you were too tired to cook at home all add up to threaten your barely-balanced budget.

We'll assume at this point that your total figure is unacceptably high, so feel free to go back over the budget and bring it more in line with what you really can afford, trimming here and there. As you do so, your philosophy about what's really important and what's not will guide you in deleting those items that don't do anything to reconcile your Christmas expectations with your Christmas reality.

The following list of ideas for trimming the cost of Christmas expenditures might help you reduce your spending. As always, remember that they are not presented as yet another roster of impossible achievements for which to strive, but as possible solutions to a particular problem.

Gifts

1. Dare to give your friends and family members something they really want, even if it doesn't cost a fortune or take months to create. Consider some of your personal possessions: that beautiful vase your sister admires; a barely-used stroller your brother and his wife could use for their new baby; a book that you have read and enjoyed and want to share with a friend; the extra sofa-bed in the den for your son who is furnishing his first apartment; a family heirloom for your children.

2. Shop garage sales and thrift shops for antiques, collectibles, and toys.

3. Send a gift to your favorite charitable organization in the name of a friend and kill two birds (gift and contribution) with one stone. Match the charity with the gift recipient's interests. Your initiative may introduce her to an organization she'll want to continue to support.

4. If your family is large, think about drawing names each year and giving to one person instead of to everyone. Or give only to your

sibling's young children, or give family gifts instead of gifts to each individual.

5. Give a gift of time and friendship, by promising to baby-sit, clean house, wallpaper a room, or provide some other needed service. Make an attractive coupon that the recipient can "redeem" sometime during the coming year.

6. A food item that is your specialty—bread, marmalade, cheese spread, fudge—makes a good gift.

7. Do you have trading stamps saved? This is the time to use them. Redeem them yourself, or swap with a friend who needs more books to get what he wants. Some people would like the stamps themselves, so they can choose their own gift.

8. Focus on one gift that you can give to several people on your list. Some gifts—crocheted hot pads, a case of homemade root beer, or cloth napkins of your own design—would be appreciated by anyone. Buy or make these in quantity to save time and money.

Christmas Greetings

1. Send your Christmas cards at a time of the year when you have more time and money. Suggestions: May Day, Valentine's Day, Midsummer's Day.

2. Forego a professional portrait and use a favorite snapshot from the preceding year to enclose in your cards.
(See PICTURES suggestions.)

3. Send Christmas postcards instead of cards with envelopes and thus greatly reduce the cost of stationery and postage.

4. Design and "quick-print" your own cards or letters; get envelopes from a stationer rather than department stores.

5. Call long-distance friends and relatives on weekends when telephone rates are lowest.

Postage & Freight

1. Plan ahead to avoid the necessity of using express-mail services to get a gift to its destination on time. Remember to send any overseas packages well ahead of time to they can take a slow boat (cheap) instead of an airplane (expensive) to their destination.

2. Compare relative costs of U.S. Mail, UPS, and other delivery services when sending packages.

3. Send cards only to out-of-town friends and relatives. Hand-deliver in-town greetings (as long as it doesn't call for a special car trip to do so).

4. Many department stores and mail-order shopping services will send your gift for you. This saves time and money, since they always find the least expensive delivery service available.

Gift Wrapping

1. Make your own wrapping paper by putting potato block prints on tissue or kraft wrapping paper. You can cannibalize grocery sacks, cutting them up to get respectable-sized sheets of paper, or decorate and use them as-is to hold gifts. This idea is especially useful for unboxed, odd-shaped, hard-to-wrap items.

2. Reuse good-quality paper and ribbons saved from previous years.

3. Wrap gifts in Sunday funnies; tie with yarn.

4. Take advantage of free gift wrapping whenever it is available. If this service is offered, you're already paying for it and might as well use it.

5. Place a large cardboard box in the basement, attic, or closet, and fill it throughout the year with items that will be useful for Christmas gift wrapping: boxes, bows, paper, packing materials, tags, stickers, funny paper—anything you can accumulate for later use.

Food & Serving

1. Borrow linen tablecloths, napkins, china dishes, centerpieces, and other seldom-used items needed for entertaining, instead of buying them. Approach a friend who has similar taste in these items with the idea of purchasing them jointly, sharing cost and ownership.

2. Many expensive table service items—punch bowls, for example—can be rented.

3. Watch for sales on food staples and expensive baking ingredients during the months before Christmas. Buy a few of these items each time you go to the grocery store in order to reduce the shock to your checkbook by spreading out the impact.

4. Borrow kitchen equipment like bundt pans, cookie sheets, spring-form pans, pasta machines, juicers, meat grinders, etc. from friends. Don't buy these things! If you decide later that you can't live without an item, put it on your Christmas want-list.

5. When you can, make casseroles ahead of time and freeze them for use on busy days, so you are less tempted to eat out when you are too rushed to make dinner.

Decorating

1. Buy or make one or two items each year that are durable and can be enjoyed from one year to the next.

2. Fresh-cut trees become less expensive as Christmas approaches. So when you can, buy late.

3. Decorate a tree with cookies and edible goodies. Most cookies can be prepared with a hole in them, or wrapped in plastic wrap and hooked onto the tree. Untrimming the tree is fun when the ornaments can be eaten.

4. Cut your own tree. Farmers often raise trees to sell at Christmastime; they usually cost less than at a tree farm or nursery.

5. Scavenge fresh greenery for wreaths and garland in your own back yard and neighborhood. Ask friends with nice evergreen trees and shrubs if you can cut some hidden boughs. Greenery gives a maximum holiday effect for a minimum amount of money.

6. Acquire wreaths that can be used for years. These may be made of pine cones, corn husks, grape vines, etc. Purchase them from local craftsmen, or try making one yourself from materials you can obtain inexpensively.

7. Make your own candles. Use old candle stubs and miscellaneous pieces for materials. Put them everywhere in the house. Use odd pieces of crockery, old drinking glasses, china saucers, and all available candleholders to display them. Group them for a dramatic effect.

8. Decorate a houseplant with ornaments instead of getting a traditional tree. Some good candidates are: Norfolk Island pine, lemon or orange trees, Arabian coffee plant or coralberry, small-leafed rubber tree, laurel tree. Use simple, lightweight ornaments so you don't harm the plant.

Pictures

1. Watch for sales on film and developing.

2. When making multiple prints for cards, have them made well ahead of time so you can take advantage of specials. If you wait too long to have your prints made, you'll end up paying a premium price for fast service or miss your deadline or—more likely—both.

Clothes

1. Add this year's accessories to last year's clothes.

2. Share your children's fancy holiday clothes with friends, and let them share with you. Little velvet suits and long satin dresses get so little wear that it's a shame not to pass them around.

3. Get one dress or suit and wear it to every event. It is unlikely that you will be seen in it more than once by anyone, since there is very little overlap of guests at holiday functions. The people at the office party won't be at your church banquet, the New Year's Day game bash, or a neighborhood cookie party. Stay away from clothing that is so obviously "Christmas" that you won't wear it any other time of the year, unless you plan to wear it year after year.

Travel

1. Combine in-town trips. Or walk; it's cheaper.

2. There are very few fare discounts available at Christmastime for air, rail, or bus travel since it's the peak travel season. Consider making your trip at some other time when it's more economical to travel.

Entertainment

1. It costs more to serve a full meal than dessert.

2. Entertain for breakfast or lunch, when the fare is not expected to be so elaborate.

3. Co-host a party with a friend, sharing cost and effort.

4. Consider a party where guests bring some of the food—a cookie exchange, for example.

5. Play "maid" at a friend's party in exchange for the same favor at yours. The maid comes early to help prepare the food and set the table, keeps the kitchen going, and cleans up afterward.

Miscellaneous Suggestions

1. Share baby-sitting favors with a friend.

2. Put off any redecorating plans until after the holiday. In addition to creating a financial strain, they take a lot of time and energy.

3. If at all possible, do your gift and grocery shopping without your young children. You are less likely to buy things you don't really want if you are free from the pressure of their demands.

4. After-Christmas sales on cards, wrapping paper, toys, decorations, and artificial trees will help cut next year's cost. It takes a lot of foresight to see how much you'll benefit from buying early, but it's well worth it.

5. Do all your shopping and celebrating later in the season. Nearly everything you will need to buy becomes less and less expensive as the 25th approaches. Even grocery items like almond bark and candied fruit go on sale when the holidays are over. Consider making your expensive fruit cake or chocolate-covered pretzels after the 25th, so you can take advantage of the sales.

Once you have your expenses at their most reasonable level (write your final figure in Column B), you must balance them with your projected income.

In the space below, write down the extra sources of money you might have that can help pay for holiday expenses.

Christmas bonus(es) $ _____

Savings at the bank earmarked for
    the holidays (Christmas Club
    account, etc.)   _____

Money under the mattress, in the
    cookie jar, etc.   _____

Overtime wages   _____

Extra part-time job   _____

Cash gifts   _____

Other: _____   _____

_____   _____

Grand Total Income $ _____

Now subtract your expenses (see page 69).   _____

Difference $ _____

Do you have more money than you'll need to get through the holidays? Congratulations!

Do you have just enough to make it through? Good! Keep a close eye on your budget, so you don't upset the balance.

Do you have more expenses than income? In that case, you will face one or more of the following:

—Overdrawn bank balance.
—Checking Plus, at interest.
—Charge card usage—with interest if you can't pay the balance by the time the bills come due.
—Unpaid bills, missed rent or house payment.
—Disappointment because you can't buy some of the things you wanted to buy (expectation/reality discrepancy).
—Dipping into savings earmarked for some other purchase (house down-payment, vacation fund, car, etc.).
—Borrowing from friends.
—Borrowing from the bank.
—Sacrificing everyday comforts for Christmas celebration.
—Something even worse.

Are you willing to pay the cost? Maybe you need to go back over your expenses and do still more cutting. Maybe you need to look at your income list and make sure you've thought of every possible source of revenue. Or you need to reconcile yourself to the fact that Christmas—Christmas expenses, that is—will continue on into the next year. I've long suspected that this is what is meant by "Christmas in July."

Time Is Money

If you are to reconcile the Christmas you want with the Christmas you get, you will need to pay close attention to the time and money aspect of your celebration.

Time isn't *actually* money, of course. It's time. And money is money. But poor planning in the time area can cost money, and inattention to the financial side of things can waste time too. They work hand in hand.

If you can organize your time with the calendar on pages 62 and 63 (or in some other efficient way), you will find that money is less likely to be wasted. And if you can work out a realistic budget—working with your spouse and anyone else who will be affected by it—you will save time as well as worry. You will know what you can spend and have at least some idea of how you are going to handle any discrepancy between what comes in and what goes out.

Now that time and money have been reckoned with, we can let the celebration begin!

Christmas Is for Kids

t is a strong belief in our culture that Christmas is for kids. We hold firm to the idea that all the foods, gifts, decorations, songs, and festivity are aimed at pleasing our children.

In support of the myth, we have a classic picture of the new father who gives his nine-month-old son an expensive Lionel train set for Christmas, claiming all along that he does it for the little guy, comically denying the fact that his son is only an excuse to finally indulge in his fantasy of being engineer of the finest locomotive in the land.

This myth that Christmas is for kids also explains why I bake dozens of fancy sugar cookies each year, elaborately decorate them, claim that they are the kids' favorites, and then eat most of them myself. Well, they'd be too sweet for the children anyway, don't you see? Tooth decay, spoiled appetites, hyperactivity . . . and my little boys aren't really old enough to appreciate all the work that's gone into them. Besides, they'd just as soon have a frosted graham cracker. So I eat nearly every one of them myself (I share a few with my friends), late in the evening, when the day's work is done, sitting in front of the lit Christmas tree, after the little rascals have been tucked snugly in their beds.

All this is fairly harmless. Our belief that Christmas is for kids allows us to let go of our adult inhibitions: we can now dress up like Santa Claus, put that chipped plaster nativity scene on the mantel one more year, hang the old stockings, play "The Little Drummer Boy" eight times a day for two weeks—all for the children, of course.

Buying into the myth becomes dangerous, however, when we saddle children with an unfair burden that requires them to rise to our occasion. Since we're doing it all for them, why aren't they more cooperative—more appreciative—more delighted? We sacrifice and plan and struggle so they can have the best possible Christmas. Why don't they see that? Why don't they want to go to Aunt Myrt's for a holiday family reunion? What would possess a child to eat all the heads—and the heads only—off twenty-six frosted gingerbread men? Why won't Jenny play with the embroidered beanbags I made her? Why is Elizabeth crying, for goodness sake?

We perpetuate the myth that Christmas is for kids in a hundred ways, and this only increases our disgust and dismay when they fail to exhibit proper respect and appreciation for everything we've done for them.

In addition to making parents, grandparents, and other doters very unhappy, many of a child's real needs are ignored. By holding to the belief that Christmas is for kids, we are likely to miss what it is that kids really *do* want from Christmas.

What is the child's Christmas fantasy? How does she see Christmas in her mind's eye? The most ready response is that what children want from Christmas is toys, toys, toys. This seems obvious. As soon as holiday television advertising campaigns commence in mid-November, parents are hounded with subtle hints, direct requests, and shameful begging: "I want a Robotank; I want a Baby-Wets-A-Lot; I love that ski outfit they have at Magee's; I could really get around this town if I had an eighteen-speed bike." The idea that *Christmas = Toys* for kids of all ages is an equation so clearly balanced that one hardly questions it.

The equation is false, however. Here is the truth: at Christmastime children want the same thing they want the rest of the year. They want to be loved; they want security; they want acceptance; they want to believe that they are wanted and that they belong.

Before we go any further, it is necessary to acknowledge the part that the various media play in provoking the "gimme" attitude children develop during the month of December. Many children, especially younger ones, are painfully suggestive when it comes to wanting whatever they see on television. It has but to flicker into view on the screen, and it becomes their heart's desire. They *must* have it, even if they don't know what it is. And if they suspect they might not get it, they are crushed. They feel woefully forsaken if they cannot have the toys they see on TV: the toys that make the kids in the commercials happy, the toys that make those same kids have lots of nice friends to play with, the toys that give those commercial kids a big new house to live in and a mother who brings cookies and Kool-Aid while they're playing with their My Little Pony dolls.

Isn't this readily apparent? I recognize in myself a tremendous response to beer ads, by way of example. I hesitate to mention it, but when I see those young, upwardly mobile young couples having a Lowenbrau, I almost believe that if I go out and buy a case, a swarm of caring, interesting, attractive friends—whom I have somehow known for years—will materialize, and we'll sit in front of our natural stone fireplace (with the hearth as big as all outdoors) on the bearskin rug, pour our liquid ambrosia into crystal schooners, and laugh and tell stories as the flickering light from the cheerful fire beams from our beautiful faces while we bask in the warm fellowship of our Rocky Mountain A-frame . . .

How much more susceptible is the six-year-old? A child whose parents are busy much of the time with their various responsibilities, a child whose red hair and freckles invite ridicule on the playground, a child who has trouble in school because he's dyslexic, a child who wishes he had a big brother instead of a colicky baby sister who has effectively upstaged him in the family circus? Of course he wants a Gobot! Naturally he'd like to have coordinated Winnie the Pooh clothes from Sears! Who wouldn't like to eat Frankenberry cereal for breakfast every morning? Obviously that's where the happiness is. The commercial kids demonstrating all these products don't have the same problems and anxieties he does. What else can he conclude?

Many parents, when confronted with their child's desire for the latest Christmas toys, feel obligated to indulge. "It's what he really wants and after all, Christmas is for kids."

So the financially-struggling parents agree not to give gifts to each other this year so that Jason can have a Snake Mountain, complete with twelve action figures that come in their own handy carrying case. They go to five different stores before they finally find one that hasn't sold out of this popular toy, happy to sacrifice for something that is "important" to their child. And on Christmas morning excited little Jason opens up the several packages, plays with the set for twenty minutes or so, and then leaves the whole mess on the living room floor, goes upstairs to his room, and takes a nap—at 9:30 in the morning.

No, children don't want toys for Christmas. They want the same things they want—but maybe don't get?—the rest of the year. When the rest of the family, especially the adults, are scurrying around baking bread, cleaning house, entertaining friends, rushing to church, and decorating the tree, then the way to feel a part of things, the way to belong, is to plug into the toys and gifts apsect of the whole thing and milk it for all it's worth. Really, what else can a kid do?

While we strive for sparkling, no-wax shines, believing that Calgon Bouquet has the power take us away from it all, our children are pinning their hopes on Mattel.

There was a time, you see, when children did not watch seven hours of television a day. They didn't wander the expansive toy department of discount stores, educating themselves on the absolute latest in fun. They didn't know that Underoos are the only kind of underwear worth having. They were totally ignorant about home computers, video games, and electronic amusements. They weren't wise to the fact that if you wrote a letter to Santa Claus and asked Dad to mail it, you would get almost everything on your want-list. As a matter of fact, Santa Claus was unheard of; there was a story about Saint Nicholas, but he was quite different than our modern-day jolly old elf whose life is built around rewarding little girls and boys for a year's good behavior with a bagful of toys.

In that not-so-long-ago time, children were an integral part of the family celebration. Little girls helped their mother bake sweet breads and cakes; the whole family marched into the woods to pick out a suitable tree to be cut and placed in the family home; young boys chopped wood with their fathers and did chores with them, giving extra portions to the animals on Christmas Eve. And when Christmas Day came, they were given a handmade doll or a book of adventure stories as a gift.

A bit romantic? Well, yes, it is. We tend to paint our own generation in the worst possible light, forgetting that each era has had its problems and disappointments. But it would be good to remember that toys and gifts have not always been the focus of Christmas celebration. And if you value simple pleasures more than Madison Avenue, then you can be assured that there are ways of turning Christmas around—or at least shifting it a little—to a place where your own values are more fairly represented, and where merchandising has less of a say in how you celebrate the anniversary of Christ's birth and the salvation of mankind.

Children cannot be bought off or put off. It takes time, patience, and determination to get things straight with your children so that you and they are celebrating Christmas together in a spirit of love and trust. Parents must not be bullied by children; children must not be ignored by parents.

Sending Messages

How can you begin? Start by deciding what message you want to relay to your child. What is it you want to tell him? What do you want to share with her?

The list of statements below verbalizes some likely messages. Write the names of children you are involved with in the columns on the right-hand side of the page, and check off the messages you would like to give those children. If something you want to say is not mentioned, then add it to the bottom of the page.

Do it now.

Christmas Messages to Children

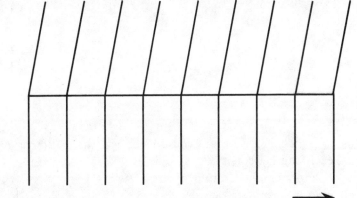

LIST NAME OF CHILDREN ABOVE COLUMN

1. You are an important person to me.
2. I am limited in how much money I can spend on you.
3. I am limited in the amount of time I can spend with you.

LIST NAME OF CHILDREN ABOVE COLUMN

 4. My energy is limited.
 5. You must learn to be a contributing member of this family.
 6. You deserve to be pampered.
 7. I love you.
 8. I am trying to love you.
 9. You need to learn how to give to others.
10. I look to you for strength.
11. You need to learn how to receive from others.
12. You can trust me.
13. I trust you.
14. I will not always be available for you.
15. You are still a child.
16. You must begin to act like an adult.
17. Christmas is a sad time for me.
18. Christmas is a happy time for me.
19. Christmas is a holy celebration.
20.
21.
22.
23.
24.
25.

Focus now on one or two messages that are most important for each child. Remember, go slow. If you say everything, you run the risk of communicating nothing. Write them here, filling in the blanks with your own message.

To _____ I wish to say _____ ,
     (child's name)   (first message)

and _____ .
     (second message)

To _____ I wish to say _____ ,
     (child's name)   (first message)

and _____ .
     (second message)

To _____ I wish to say _____ ,
     (child's name)   (first message)

and _____ .
     (second message)

To _____ I wish to say _____ ,
     (child's name)   (first message)

and _____ .
     (second message)

To _____ I wish to say _____ ,
     (child's name)   (first message)

and _____ .
     (second message)

In some instances you may be able to simply sit down and tell the child his message. A single parent of a fourteen-year-old boy may indeed be able to say to her child, "Jim, I need for you to know that Christmas is a very sad time for me ever since your father died. I loved him very much and I miss him, especially at times like this. I also want you to know that I love you very, very much."

Or a parent might say to a five-year-old, "I know that's a very nice toy. I understand that. You should know that toys like that cost a great deal of money. I'd get it for you if I could, but it costs more money than I have. I'm sorry about that."

Or, "Yes, I could buy you that toy. But I'm not going to, because it represents something that I think is bad. In our family we don't think that guns are toys, and that's why you cannot have a G.I. Joe Bazooka."

More often, the messages we give to children are most effectively communicated in other ways—through what we do, for example.

Parents who require each child in the family to be responsible for certain household chores are saying, "You must learn to be a contributing member of this family." The mother who brings a glass of 7-Up to her sick child says, "You deserve special attention." The teenager who listens to her little sister's account of what happened at school today is saying, "I am concerned." And the stepparent who attends a Little League game with her husband's son is saying, "I am trying to love you more."

How can important messages be communicated to children in a Christmas setting? If we fail to clearly define the messages we wish to send, both for ourselves and for the child, we may communicate something that is harmful for both of us. Your decision to give a message to a particular child indicates your willingness to hear that message yourself. If you want to tell Carole that she is important to you, then you need to realize it yourself—admit how much she means in your life. If you believe the message sincerely, then you can communicate it to the child.

I cannot tell you how to give a message to a child, other than to remind you that what you do is generally more credible than what you say; that you must believe it yourself before anyone else will; that there are no shortcuts or escape hatches.

In the space below, you can brainstorm ways in which you will deliver your messages. Along with respect for each child's individuality and the importance of what you have to say, explore possible avenues of communication. Here are some examples:

"I want to tell Sean that he must learn how to give to others. I will do this by suggesting ways he can earn money to buy presents for family members, and by taking him with me when I deliver cookies to the shut-ins on our block."

"I want to tell Kristin that my energy is limited. I will do this by involving her in filling out my Christmas planning calendar, and by asking her to assume additional housecleaning responsibilities during the month of December."

"I want to tell my grandson Robbie that I am limited in the amount of time I can spend with him because of my job. I will do this by sending him a card saying how much I miss him, and inviting him to spend a week with me next summer when school is over for both of us."

Now work on your statements, exploring avenues of communication for what you have to say:

I want to tell _____ _____ .
       (child's name)   (the message)
I will do this by _____ , _____ ,
_____ , and/or _____ .

I want to tell _____ _____ .
       (child's name)   (the message)
I will do this by _____ , _____ ,
_____ , and/or _____ .

I want to tell _____ _____ .
       (child's name)   (the message)
I will do this by _____ , _____ ,
_____ , and/or _____ .

I want to tell _____ _____ .
       (child's name)   (the message)
I will do this by _____ , _____ ,
_____ , and/or _____ .

I want to tell _____ _____ .
       (child's name)   (the message)
I will do this by _____ , _____ ,
_____ , and/or _____ .

I want to tell _____ _____ .
       (child's name)   (the message)
I will do this by _____ , _____ ,
_____ , and/or _____ .

In sending messages to children, you might entertain the following suggestions. Consider incorporating one or more (not too many, remember!) into this year's celebration:

—Substitute seasonal reading for the regular fare at bedtime or storytime. Longer books (some of which are mentioned in Chapter Three) can be read a chapter a night throughout the holidays.

—Tell your children stories about your own past Christmases at bedtime and storytime. The stories can relate your disappointments as well as your joys. You might, for example, recount a time when you wanted a particular toy very badly for Christmas and didn't get it. Discuss with your child how you felt, how you reacted, etc. Such a discussion might help her deal with a disappointment that she's facing this year. This is also a good time to describe family customs, detailing how they came to be a part of the present-day celebration.

—The flurry of Christmas activity is often upsetting to children. Try, as much as possible, to keep *some* routine throughout the season so the child isn't totally befuddled. Routine is important in the same way tradition is: it's a landmark, something to steer by. Maintaining the same order of events regarding bedtime, household responsibilities, and behavior standards is important to a child— even if the routine isn't heartily endorsed per se. You might think it would be a nice "treat" to let your child off the hook when it comes to practicing the piano or taking the Wednesday night bath because it is, after all, Christmas. But this could be upsetting to your child, who loses an important contact point in his life and wonders now if anything goes. Rules concerning "what happens when" make Christmas celebrations, which are very much out of the ordinary, seem more familiar, more predictable, and less frantic—for children as well as adults.

—Even young children can be taught the joy of giving during Christmas. Here's a good tradition: on Christmas Eve, let your child pick a toy from his/her collection, explaining that it will be placed under the Christmas tree (or beside the fireplace) and that Santa will collect it when he comes, giving it in turn to some other child who would like it. You might be surprised at the toy that your child

Relaying the Message

chooses. Toddlers and youngsters who have no financial resources of their own (and consequently limited opportunities to share) often will pick their very favorite doll or truck to give the other, unknown child. Even the smallest gesture helps the child understand that when he receives, it is because someone else gave. (Remember, it is your responsibility to give the gift-toy to a needy child.)

—There's no substitute for time spent with children. The concept of "quality time" has some merit, but it should be remembered that there has to be a certain *quantity* of time available for children as well. Children are often neglected and left to themselves when holiday preparation and celebration is in full force. Remember your children. Remember to spend time with them.

—"Some assembly required" toys should be assembled prior to opening. Kids hate to wait for Dad to put a thing together when they're anxious to play.

—Wrap children's gifts with a thought as to how they will be unwrapped. A glued or stapled-shut corrugated cardboard box, wrapping paper applied with yards of cellophane tape and tied up with a stout piece of twine or ribbon, shrink-wrap packaging, and impenetrable plastic bags all have the power to put an excited little child into tears of frustration.

Don't let the container ruin the fun of the gift. Remove problematic manufacturer's packaging and re-wrap with the child in mind. Or add a bow and don't wrap it at all.

—Allow kids to open their gifts at their own pace. Some presents are real show-stoppers, and should be allowed to do just that. Several years ago my niece got a nice little set of doll dishes from her mother, my nephew conveniently got a four-pack of Play-Doh, and they decided to halt the entire gift-opening ceremony by having a tea party right then and there on the coffee table. With several gifts yet to go, they merrily created petit fours and enjoyed imaginary hot chocolate.

It's pointless to get impatient and hurry a child along to his next gift, just because you're anxious to see the expression on his face when he opens it or you're anxious to cut the coffee cake. Let the enjoyment last and last. This is Christmas. You've waited all year for it. Don't be in such a hurry.

—Christmas can become a rite of passage when you give a gift of freedom and, consequently, responsibility to your child. Children and teenagers will appreciate such gifts as:

• an extended weekend curfew.
• no more bedtime. (Accompany this gift with a reliable alarm clock that the child can use to get himself up in the morning.)
• a set of keys to the family car, and resultant privileges to use the car.
• a handful of "You can count on me" phone call coupons. Each coupon entitles your teenager to a no-questions-asked ride home when he or she gets in a tough situation (at a party where friends have been drinking, when your child has been drinking, when ditching a bad date—who knows?) Tape a couple of dimes to each coupon for phone money. Are you ready to give this gift? If you do, you must be absolutely sure that you are willing to respect your child's right to tell you nothing.

Freedom gifts are sometimes very difficult to give, and equally hard to receive. When they are given formally, though, at Christmas, they tend to be respected and used wisely.

—Plan to spend some time in the days after Christmas writing thank-you notes with your child. A parent can help a child realize at an early age that the important and pleasurable part of receiving gifts is to acknowledge them. Little ones can dictate thank-you's, older children can write their own notes with help, and teenagers can take full responsibility for procuring notepaper, stamps, and mailing the notes themselves. If there has been any disappointment on the child's part about what he didn't get, a nice-sized pile of thank-yous should help him refocus on what he *did* receive. Set a good example by writing your own thank-yous promptly, including one to your own child for all the nice things she said, did, and gave.

—Fred Rogers (television's "Mr. Rogers") suggests that when a child has a long list of toys she wants for Christmas, the parent might consider giving the child the #1 wish from the list (if feasible) to demonstrate that he is sensitive to what the child wants, and then feel free to disregard items #2 through #37 in favor of what the parent wants the child to have. This might be a good way to recognize the wants of the child, and yet resist the dictates of a demanding kid.

—If your child wants a toy that you absolutely cannot or will not give, offer something in the way of an explanation well before gift-opening time, so that the child doesn't build up expectations that cannot possibly be realized. It's better to say, right from the start, "No, Billy, I'm absolutely not going to give you a condominium in Malibu for Christmas" than to make him sift eagerly through his presents for the deed on Christmas morning.

Christmas is for kids? Sure it is. It's also for parents, the elderly, the poor, and the alone. It is for Christ, in appreciation of his wonderful gift. A child who finds his place in Christmas along with his family, friends, and community will be happier than the one who is mistakenly led to believe that he is the star of the show on December 25.

But what about the rest of the family? Read on . . .

Box A— A Word About Santa Claus

Some parents completely reject any mention of Santa Claus as a Christmas personage, while others go to great lengths keeping the story alive for their children. Which is the right path?

Only you can decide. Your own childhood experiences will undoubtedly influence your decision. If Santa Claus was a wonderful part of Christmas for you, and if your eventual knowledge that he was a myth wasn't a traumatic disappointment, you may want to foster the same fantasy for your own children. Any other experience, particularly a huge crisis when you learned The Truth About Santa, will change your outlook.

I have no hard data to inform this discussion, no definitive word from a panel of experts as to whether or not it's good to encourage children to believe in Santa Claus. I came from a family in which he was recognized as a fictional character only; Christmas was very much a religious holiday in my childhood home. Santa did not bring gifts and was not part of our household decorations; we didn't eat Santa Claus cookies or hang up stockings for him to fill. We didn't get gifts from Santa, or sing "You better watch out . . ." From an early age I was aware that because we were Christians, Christmas was a different kind of holiday for us than it was for my friends or the kids at school. I understood and accepted that.

I would offer the following thoughts for your consideration as you decide how the question will be handled for you and the children you care about.

1. The parent should set the standard. If you are a grandparent, aunt, or uncle, check with the child's parents to see what they are telling the child and what the child believes. Reinforce that, even if you don't agree. Unless you are the parent or guardian, you should not decide the issue. Similarly, the mother and father must reach an agreement between themselves on how the matter will be presented.

2. Remember that a child's mind is not neatly divided into fact and fantasy areas. They merge. What would be called psychosis in an adult (imaginary friends, hearing voices, wild fantasizing) is absolutely normal for the average preschool-age child.

Children are able to live fantasy at the same time that they are breathing reality. In a very strange way it is possible for a child to believe in Santa with all her heart, yet understand intuitively that he isn't "for real." As adults, we're so far removed from this kind of whimsy that it's hard for us to understand and accept it, but that's truly the way it is with kids.

3. Santa Claus can occupy his proper place as fairy tale, a make-believe character. This is his due. It is only when he is given the status of a flesh-and-blood human being that he becomes a lie.

4. It is probably not a good idea to have a child's important gifts coming from Santa Claus. The child who gets everything

from Santa remains unaware that it is his loving parents, family, and friends who have saved, shopped, created, planned, and wrapped something special for him. The deeper relationship that accompanies a child's appreciation is lost when his thanks belong to someone who cannot receive them.

5. Children who begin to question Santa's existence are sometimes told that if they quit believing in Santa, they won't get presents anymore.

This is unfair. Children deserve to have their doubts taken seriously. The child who begins to question is entitled to an honest answer. The answer can be somewhat ambiguous so the child has space to draw conclusions he can accept. For example.

"Mommy, on the playground today the big kids were saying that there isn't a Santa Claus. Is that true?"

"What do you think?"

"I don't know."

"Do you want to believe in Santa?"

"I guess so. I think the kids are right, though."

In a conversation like this, noncommittal (yet honest) feedback from the parent can help the child arrive at his own answers to his question.

Children should never be bullied into believing. To speak of withholding presents is to threaten the child with deprivation—material and emotional—if he insists on growing and developing naturally. Sooner or later she will understand that her parents lied to her, and such a deception may not be easily forgiven.

The Santa Claus issue should be carefully thought out by each parent, especially those to whom spiritual things are the crux of the Christmas celebration. My brother's little boy, upon learning that there was no Santa Claus, concluded, "Then Jesus isn't real either." His father told him decisively that Jesus *was* real and convinced him of the fact, but decided later that the fun of creating Santa Claus for his child wasn't worth the false conclusion that his son came to about Jesus.

If you perpetuate the Santa Claus myth beyond its ability to delight the child, you risk a breach in your relationship with the youngster and may certainly divert his attention from the more important values of Christmas.

Box B— A Birthday Party for Jesus

Children will enjoy having a birthday party for Jesus during the Christmas season. By celebrating the nativity in this familiar way, little children (and older ones too) will be able to understand the truth about Christmas in a way they can readily understand and accept.

The party can be given any time during the season. Some parents find that having it after December 25 helps to ease the letdown after the holidays, gives the party a relaxed time in which to happen, and fills the gap between Christmas and New Year's when children are out of school and out of celebration.

Here are some ideas:

1. Encourage the child(ren) to take an active part in planning the party and in making it happen. Involve the child in making and sending invitations, decorating the home, choosing games and activities, and preparing food. One of the chief goals of such a party is to give the child a place where she can plug into the Christmas celebration. The child's involvement is very important.

2. Birthday parties suggest presents. Each guest may be asked to bring a gift to the party that can be used for some good purpose—cookies for the elderly in a neighborhood nursing home, money that will be donated to charity, toys for needy children. Part of the festivities could include delivering the gifts to their recipients. Christ said that whatever we do for

others has been done for him. A gift to some worthwhile cause or brother in need will be understood by the child as a gift to Jesus. This is a wonderful concept to grasp early in life.

3. Suggested activities include:

—An adult or older child can read the Christmas story to the guests.

—Guests can draw the name of a nativity character from a hat, and then the entire group can act out the Christmas story. Use simple props such as a yardstick (shepherd's staff), paper hats (Wise Men's crowns), cloth headdress (Mary and Joseph), or placards to identify the players. Have a baby doll that can be used for the Christchild. The actors can pantomime the appropriate actions while someone reads the Christmas story, or can work from a prepared script. If the whole thing gets a little crazy, as it is bound to do, enjoy the fun, reflecting on how strange the first Christmas must have seemed. Young children will enjoy hearing stories of their own birth experiences as they are contrasted with Christ's birth too.

—The local public library will have many volumes of simple Christmas plays that can be enacted at your party.

—Pin-the-Tail-on-Mary's-Donkey would be an appropriate game!

—Birthday party goodies might reflect the culture that Christ was born into. Serve foods that Jesus would have eaten (or reasonable facsimiles): raisins, homemade bread, crackers, dates, nuts, olives, any kind of fruit.

Keep the party as simple as it needs to be so that the children remember its purpose—to celebrate Jesus' birthday. Many children look forward to the party as a yearly event of great importance, the focus of their holiday festivities.

6

A Time for Family

e'll assume that you took the advice in Chapter Four and consulted your family on the kind of holiday you want and listened to their suggestions and concerns about what they wanted. If you thought you could skip that step and still have a wonderful family experience at Christmastime, I caution you to rethink that assumption. By virtue of the fact that you are now reading Chapter 6 of this book, you are—believe me, you *are*—light-years ahead of your family. They may intuitively sense something wrong (or something right) with past celebrations, but it's highly unlikely that they have articulated their concerns to themselves, much less to another person. And a conscious recognition is essential to change.

With that final admonition, we continue—assured that you have spoken with your family, received feedback, and reached some sort of agreement about what you're aiming for in terms of holiday celebration this year. We're not talking about unanimous acclamation, just a general consensus. So on we go.

. . . The Rest of the Family

"I planned a big dinner for St. Stephen's Day (December 26). At 5:50 (dinner was announced for 6:00), Richard's dad said he was going for a walk; before I could stop him, he escaped out the back door. When we saw him again at 6:20, he had walked over to the 7-11, picked up a six-pack of beer, and eaten a medium-sized bag of potato chips on the way back. And these were the people that we *begged* to spend the holidays with us!"

"Our oldest boy, James, went away to college last fall. Well, he came home from school a couple of days before Christmas with the announcement that his girlfriend's family (whom we have not met) had a condominium in Ft. Walton Beach, and that they were picking him up at noon Christmas Day to spend a week there. Can you believe it? Virginia didn't know what to say, started crying, and just checked out of the whole thing. I explained to James that his mother and I had been looking forward to having him around some, that we had missed him a lot during the school year. He claimed that he was spending Christmas with us—and of course technically he was—and that he didn't see what the big deal was. We decided to let him go, but it put a damper on everything we did, both before and after he left."

"My mom and her sister haven't spoken to each other for eight years. Aunt Irene had lived with us after my dad died, but she and Mom didn't get along at all. Things got worse and worse until finally Aunt Irene left. Mom never forgave her for some of the things Irene said. Anyway, they don't talk now. I'd love to have them both over for Christmas, but every year we have to go through this complicated song-and-dance so that they won't run into each other. Aunt Irene came over with a fruitcake when Mom was here a few days ago, and you could feel the ice in the air. I've tried to talk to them about it, but it doesn't do any good. It ruins Christmas for me."

"Last year my kids' father called to say that he was going to fly in from San Diego on December 28 and take them all skiing. He didn't ask if it was okay with me, he just announced it. But I thought, 'Well, okay. He hardly ever sees them. They need their father. If he wants to take them skiing, so much the better. I can deal with it.' Of course, he never showed. I guess I wanted to believe he'd come as much as the kids did, but I know him better than they do and I should have seen the writing on the wall. He didn't send the flight number like he said he would, and we couldn't reach him by phone—no answer. He just didn't show. I didn't know what to tell the kids. What could I say? I hate that man."

"We could write a book about the problems of the so-called 'blended family,' but after six years of marriage we'd still only be able to state the problem, not provide any solutions. Between Eddie and me, we have five kids. I'm a widow, and my former husband's parents and brothers still like to be involved in what's happening with the kids—and rightly so. Eddie's ex-wife, who didn't even fight for the kids at the time of their divorce, all of a sudden has to be involved in everything. I know she wants them back now.

"The kids get along okay, I suppose. The biggest adjustments have been made. But when Christmas rolls around, it's like we're back to square one. For example, we have *three* trees. My kids have one in the basement, an old pink aluminum thing that their dad bought them years ago. Eddie's girls have their own tree upstairs—they won't have anything to do with the aluminum one. They decorate theirs really nice, make ornaments for it every year. It's really pretty, and they keep it in the living room. But the competition between those kids! Eddie and I have ours in our bedroom, with ornaments that we've bought together. We feel that we need it to affirm that we do have a relationship of our own amongst all this. We have to put each kid's presents under his or her tree, and end up having gift-opening in two rooms in the house.

"Am I being indulgent to put up with all this? I don't know. I really don't know. The thing with the trees is like a symbol; it symbolizes the fact that we're not really a family yet, that we're still torn apart in a dozen places, that we haven't come to grips with our family situation. After six years you'd think it'd be better. Really, we could write a book . . ."

"I'm what they call a 'noncustodial' parent, which is another way of saying that I never get to see my kids. So I have ten days a year when I can do everything I want to do with my kids—Christmas. And we do it! They come to my place, and we have a ball. I take them shopping for Christmas gifts. They pick out what they want to give their friends, their mom, and each other, and then we have a big gift-wrapping party the first evening. I go back the next day and buy them what they wanted for themselves. We always cut our own tree and get out all the old decorations we've made together or bought and have a great time. But all the time I know that the clock is ticking, and it's just a matter of days before they go home and I don't see them for another year.

"But we have the best time we can, do as much as we can. We try to have our own traditions. When they leave I can hardly function for a few days, and I'm seriously depressed for about a month. Then I can start looking forward to next year. Christmas is my life, because it's my kids. And what do I get for my trouble? Their mother calls me up and complains over the phone that I'm spoiling them, that it's unfair of me to give them so much when she can't, and how would I like it if she made me look like a cheapskate, and it's easy for me I only have to put up with them for ten days, she has to deal with them all year, it's not easy being a single parent, blah, blah, blah. You don't know what I go through."

Blended, extended, single-parent families—special circumstances call for special plans when it comes to the matter of families at Christmas.

Problems in the Extended Family

When one adds to the nuclear family (Mom, Dad, two kids, and Fido) a couple sets of grandparents, a few aunts and uncles, a great-grandparent or two, assorted cousins, brothers and sisters, the result is a tremendously complicated Christmas production whose choreography challenges the stability of even the very sane.

The way you handle the extended family matter will, of course, be unique, just as your family is unique. However, you might try to apply some of these suggestions to your situation:

1. Include as many extended family members in your family council meeting (see Chapter Four) as you can. If they will be participating in your celebration in any significant way, let them have some input.

2. Try to be realistic about your family. When family members possess especially disgusting personality traits or behave in particularly offensive ways, it's tempting to forget from one year to the next how awful they really are. It's always nice to give someone the benefit of a doubt, but if you are unrealistic about their strengths

and weaknesses, you may face big disappointment when you are once again reminded of how trying they are. File away for future use such information as: Mom has always thought I was a lousy parent; Bill is apt to pick a fight; Claire is super-messy and makes a wreck out of any room that she's in for more than ten minutes; George can't stand kids.

Don't despise your loved ones for their quirks and traits; just recognize the situation for what it is so you can work with it. Then you can plan to be stalwart in the face of Mom's criticisms, keep Bill away from Esther (who is also combative), ask Claire if she wouldn't like to stay at the Holiday Inn instead of sleeping on the sofa-bed in the living room, and give George plenty of space where the kids are concerned.

3. Avoid clandestine maneuvering to solve old family disputes. It may seem like a good play to trick Merle and Curtis into attending the same party in hopes that they'll settle their differences in the spirit of the season, but it's probably a bad move. For one thing, you run the risk of turning your otherwise nice occasion into a donny-brook as the two once again confront their differences. Likewise, you may expand existing rifts since the objects of your reconciliation will be put on the defensive and are likely to reject other attempts in the future.

4. Know your physical and emotional limitations when it comes to dealing with your extended family. Challenge yourself to be more accepting and more loving, but at the same time admit your own weaknesses and work with them.

Since Christmas is often the occasion for a family reunion, there are issues like who stays with whom, where meals will be eaten, and when the whole shebang will take place. Few people have a grand enough home to comfortably house their entire extended family or enough money to put everyone up at the Ritz and eat all meals out. So there must be planning, sacrifice, compromise, pa-tience, and good humor to survive the decided-upon sleeping and eating arrangements.

You may *need* to send the bunch to McDonalds for supper one night instead of fixing yet another family meal for thirteen, even if the thought of hamburgers offends your culinary sensibilities and you can't afford it anyway. You might *need* to forego exchanging gifts one year so everyone can spend that money on travel expenses, even though you'd like to do both.

Don't be afraid to admit that you're not up to the whole bunch. They're your family; you didn't get a chance to pick who was part of it. If there are some struggles in the relationships, proceed with the knowledge that you are not alone.

The Challenge of the Blended Family

The challenge of the blended family centers around children in almost every case—they are what makes it blended. When divorce is a part of the situation, there is often competition between parents for the affection of their children. The possibility that four or more sets of grandparents each want to spend some special time with the children is also a challenge. And while newly-married parents are struggling to make their relationship work, their children may be following an agenda of their own, one that does not include any plan to become part of this new arrangement.

Children, although they are surprisingly adaptable and resilient, are like adults in that they will tolerate only so much change. While change is the essence of growth, it must be approached with patience and sensitivity. The best kinds of changes are those that can occur gradually, thoughtfully, and optimistically. Children often resent changes that are forced on them as an accommodation to their parents' fulfillment. A child of a blended family will wonder why *he* has to adapt himself to all sorts of turmoil just because Mom decided to remarry.

How strongly can I stress the value of a family planning meeting? In the case of a blended family, it is doubly important to meet specifically for the purpose of ironing out the difficulties that are bound to come with the celebrating of Christmas. My personal feeling is that in the case of a blended family, such a planning meeting's purpose would be more to focus on the children's needs than the parent's wishes. The children are likely (in most cases) to have needs greater than those of the parents, and should receive first consideration.

This is not to say that children in a blended family (or any family!) should be allowed to tyrannize their parents and siblings with untoward demands. Not at all. But in the main, children—who are helpless to alter their environment (in this case, to effect a radical change in their primary support group—their family)—deserve an advocate, an understanding parent who will act as mediator between them and what they may perceive as a cruel world.

Once parents know the needs of the children, they must assume the responsibility of informing others—noncustodial parents, grandparents, the rest of the extended family—about the game plan. They must protect the children from harmful influences and activities (however well-intentioned) and be the child's representative to the rest of the family.

Grandparents in the blended family suffer too. Many have seen their children go through painful separations and bitter divorces or lost a child to death; and on top of all that, they must deal with the remarriage of their child and his/her spouse, and then share grandchildren with two other new sets of grandparents. At Christmastime the fight for the youngsters' affection and attention may be pursued by his natural parents, each parents' new spouse, his grandparents by his natural parents, his step-grandparents, in addition to a host of other relatives: aunts, uncles, step-aunts, step-uncles, cousins, step-cousins—incredible!

Grandparents who wish to avoid this mad dash may opt to forego their Christmastime "rights" and decide instead to make another time of the year their special time together with the grandchildren—perhaps the child's birthday, or the summer when she's out of school and would relish the extra attention.

Off-season celebrations can be promised with a certificate—wrapped and placed under the tree, so the child doesn't feel forgotten. Such a promise could lessen the confusion and hard feelings that are bound to occur when competing (albeit loving) relatives fight for their rightful place during the holiday season.

When it comes to reconciling dissimilar traditions and customs, deciding which ones will be retained, which will be forfeited, and which will be modified, negotiation between family members must be utilized.

For example, it may be negotiated that this year we'll go to Grandma Stuart's house for Christmas dinner, and next year go to Grandma and Grandpa Whitley's; this year we'll exchange gifts with only "real" brothers and sisters, and next year we'll get together with "steps" for a gift-exchange, and perhaps the year after that we'll all give gifts to each other; you'll spend Christmas Eve with your father, Christmas Day with your mother.

The decisions that have to be made are often painful, but they cannot be ignored. If tough problems are avoided, they will be resolved by default. It's almost always better to be intentional in knowing what your options are and decide between them as a family, recognizing the trade-offs involved and the possible consequences—in advance.

Negotiation is not a win or lose game. It's a way of solving problems. If you are interested in learning more about it, and using what you learn to have a merry Christmas with your family (I hope you are!), read *Getting to Yes* by Fisher and Ury (see the bibliography for publishing information). This book details the mediation/negotiation process and is an excellent resource for blended families (or any family) facing rough issues.

Discord in the Immediate Family

It is at Christmas that problems which have been simmering for an entire year boil over and scorch what is hoped by one and all will be an occasion to heal old wounds and restore broken family relationships to wholeness.

It's too bad Christmas can't do that. There are some poignant stories and television specials that say it is within the power of Christmas to magically transform a family, but, alas, they're just TV fantasies.

Under certain circumstances a plethora of activities, presents, and food can disguise existing problems, but inevitably there is a break in the frantic merrymaking and the difficulties emerge. Whether it is something as heartbreaking as a loveless marriage or as normal as an infant who won't sleep through the night, problems in the family tend to be exacerbated as the holidays approach and are celebrated.

Since you are the one reading this book, you are the most likely agent of change. What can you do? Can you destroy your teenage son's constant companion—his Walkman radio? Can you change your wife's eating habits? Can you heal your father of heart disease? Can you give your daughter beauty so she'll have more confidence?

While it's tempting to answer, "Yes—I can at least try!" to such questions, the truth is that attempts to change another person are nearly always unsuccessful. Even when it looks as if a change has been made, it tends to be superficial in character. In reality, *the only person you can change is yourself.*

That's right—the only person you can change is yourself. You can bully people into certain behaviors, you can rant and rave and cry and try to make people feel guilty about who they are and what they do, or you can explain rationally and clearly why they should be different, put them on a ten-step program of change, and read them self-help books by the carload. But when all is said and done, the only person you can change is *you.*

We all want to take issue with that statement, because most of us are convinced that if only someone else would change, our problems would be over. As logical as that seems on a theoretical level—indeed, as true as it is—it does not work itself out on the practical level. The pragmatic person understands that he cannot change another person; he can only change himself. Once you have gotten over your disbelief and disappointment about that fact, you are ready to do something about discord in your family and set about the task of creating a more satisfying, joyous, and value-centered Christmas for yourself and your family.

To deal with discord in the immediate family, you must go back to the plan of attack outlined in Chapter One, which is, Revise your expectations and/or revise your reality.

1. **Revise your expectations.** Assess your family situation as it is. Admit the financial difficulties, communication problems, disaffec-

tion between family members, apathy, broken relationships, old scripts, personality problems, illnesses of the body, spirit, or mind, and anything else that is an obstacle to healthy family relationships and living. Now revise your expectations in light of this data. What is realistic?

2. Revise your reality. Revise your reality by exploring avenues of change within yourself.

What's wrong with the following statements?

"This year we simply won't have fights about everything, as we have in the past."

"I'll let Byron know that I expect him to be on hand to help me run errands, and that way I won't get so frazzled."

"Connie will just have to understand that we're not made out of money."

Such resolves place the burden on others—such as Byron and Connie—to clean up *their* act. The speakers are assuming that another person will be willing and able to change. While miracles do happen, I wouldn't count on it.

What's different about the following statements?

"I will be more understanding and less critical; I won't take offense—especially when none is intended—and will do everything in my power to keep things upbeat and positive."

"Since Byron is no help at all with running errands, I'll plan my own trips more carefully so they don't take up so much time."

"I will go over my Christmas budget with Connie and show her what my limits are."

In each case, the possibility exists that Byron and Connie will get the message that is being conveyed, but the main responsibility

rests on the speaker to do what he/she can do to revi.
When you decide to take responsibility for what *you* can do, things
can happen—things can change!

The nice payoff from concentrating on your own behavior is
that others are often inspired by your show of good faith and
resolve to do something themselves. Your good example gives them
ideas and a willingness to change and makes them more receptive to
finding means by which they, too, can adjust and adapt.

The Single Parent Family

One child in five lives in a single-parent home. In a very special
sense, single parents are aware of the difference between the Christmas celebrated by themselves and their children and the Norman
Rockwell standard that is set before them. By virtue of the fact that
their marriage has ended in death, separation, or divorce, they are
unequipped to create The Ideal Christmas.

Realizing this, they feel pressured into overcompensating for
the fact that their children have lost a parent or are the victims of a
broken home by lavishing an inordinate amount of energy, attention, and money on their children in an attempt to make up for the
hard blows received. Noncustodial parents especially have a terrific
opportunity—and face a terrific temptation—to cram a year's worth
of affection into a few days, and this is often resented by the
custodial parent who in addition to being alone over the holidays
feels subjected to an unfair comparison by his or her child.

Some parents try to protect the child from his situation, pretending that Daddy will come back when Daddy surely will not.
Separated or divorced couples sometimes reunite for the holidays
rather than face the prospect of "sharing" their children during
Christmas; husband and wife move in together under the same roof
and try to pretend that they are happily married again and that the
whole horrible breakup never occurred.

Faced with believing the myth that "Christmas is for kids,"
single parents—most of whom have full-time, out-of-the-home
jobs—are pressured into spending time, money, and energy they
don't have creating "quality time" with their kids, when what they

may really need is to get out of the house or get away from their children, for a time at least, and take care of their own needs.

Single parents who have dealt with all these frustrations offer the following pieces of advice that may help others make it through the often-painful holidays in one piece.

1. Admit to your children that you will have a hard time with Christmas. This doesn't mean that you place a burden upon shoulders too slight to bear it, or that you should involve small children excessively in your pain. But they can know that you are unhappy or lonely, as they are.

2. At some point in their lives children will have to deal with their own disappointments as far as the broken family situation is concerned. The absent father who doesn't send a card or gift cannot be protected by you forever. Your child must eventually find his own way of interpreting such behavior; she must come to grips with a neglectful parent or face the finality of a parent's death in his own way. As a parent, you may feel that you should step in and spare the child as much grief as possible. But grieving—whether for a parent who has died or for a family that is broken by divorce—must be carried out individually. You cannot do it for your child, nor should you try.

3. In the case of noncustodial parents, a buy-off will quickly be recognized for what it is. The parent who ignores his or her child all year will hardly be excused for such neglect just because he or she comes through with a lot of expensive toys or exciting trips. The complaint of custodial parents is that the hard part of raising a child is the day-to-day parenting. Children soon realize that this is true too. They may cling to extravagances if that's all they're likely to get from a noncustodial parent, but they're wise to it just the same.

4. Although you might feel pressured to spend a lot of time with your children at Christmas, remember that you have needs too. Don't be afraid to accept an invitation to a party without your kids, or to get some time by yourself during the holidays. You're going to need it.

5. Time spent with the extended family often takes some of the bite out of being a single parent. If you can get together with your family, your former spouse's family, with your children's grandparents, with your brothers and sisters, you will have more support, a fuller house, and more help in celebrating Christmas.

6. Similarly, you might want to spend the holidays with other single-parent families you know. Pool your kids for a Waltons effect. Admit—perhaps for the first time?—that you are definitely single now. Celebrate the fact that you're a survivor.

7. You don't have to confront all your problems and disappointments at Christmas. If your loss is very recent, don't feel that you have to plow through the holidays like a trooper, dealing with all the pain. You don't have to prove anything. You can modify your celebration so that it's in line with your mood and your abilities. It's okay to take some shortcuts, to gloss over some sore spots, if it helps you and your children have a meaningful celebration in which Christ's birth is remembered and honored.

8. Think it through carefully before you decide to get together with a husband or wife from whom you are separated or divorced for the holidays. Such reunions are nearly always painful for everyone involved and only serve to underline the fact that serious problems are present in the relationship. Although loneliness makes it tempting to try for some sort of reconciliation—even a brief one—Christmas is probably not the time to tackle it. Save your efforts for some other time of the year when they're likely to be more fruitful.

Sharing Families

It is often rewarding to share family celebrations. The person who feels alone during the holidays can be helped through a difficult time by plugging into a ready-made family celebration. And those who have an existing family structure in which to work can often share with others, as when single parents merge families, or the extended family gets together.

If you have a good thing going with your family Christmas, by all means share it! Share it with someone you love, or with someone who needs to be loved.

Who needs your celebration? Here are some possibilities: a close friend who will be alone for the holidays; a neighbor you'd like to get to know better; an older person at a nursing home who has no friends or relatives; a foreign student; a needy family in your community; a young couple from church; a family like yours.

Once you have decided who it is that you want to share with, you can examine the components of your celebration and find a place where a guest could plug in. You could share holiday baking with a shut-in, your Christmas Eve dinner with a neighbor who has to work on Christmas Day, your extra bedroom with a foreign student who cannot stay in the dorm over semester break, Christmas Day with a friend who has lost her husband.

Some families wonder whether they will lose the intimacy or the magic of their celebration by including "strangers" in it. While this is a possibility, it is more likely that your happiness will be increased with the addition of people who are grateful for your invitation to participate. Be sure your invitations come from the entire family—that is, that by way of a family council, mealtime discussion, or whatever, everyone is in agreement that so-and-so should be asked to come over at a certain time for a certain function.

In inviting others to celebrate with you, you needn't open *every* family activity. Keep for your immediate family the most intimate moments, and share others.

Will you be uncomfortable? Will you have to be on your best behavior? Will they feel welcome? Will they have fun? Will they appreciate the gesture? Will they like the food? Will they become obnoxious?

You won't know until you try it. When I was a little girl, our dinner table always seemed to have at it one or a dozen people that Dad had brought home from work with him—an old friend in town for a couple of days, a visiting missionary, or a new family at church. I remember one eccentric old lady—Mrs. Diver—that he invited over for Sunday dinner shortly after accepting the pastorate of a new church. She had decidedly purple hair, I remember, and was rather crazy in a number of ways. She enthusiastically accepted the invitation for dinner and while at the table monopolized the conversation with the most fantastic ramblings, talking about everything under the sun in a very bizarre way. I think she even spilled her water. And then she said, at the end of what, for our family, had been an exhausting hour, "You know, I've been attending this church for three years, and this is the first time I've ever been in the home of anyone else who goes to it."

We could have cried. It explained everything. We were so glad that we'd had her over.

Strange things might happen when you invite someone into your home, especially if it's someone you don't know well or someone who is struggling with big issues. But the potential for satisfaction is great. Something wonderful could happen too!

You must decide if you're willing to take the risk. You, and the rest of your family, must determine if you are in a place where opening the doors to your home or sharing your celebration with someone else is the right thing to do. It may not be. But it is always possible that the person you welcome into your home may be like a young couple many years ago who desperately needed a place to stay while visiting a foreign town, and who were finally offered meager hospitality—a stable—by an innkeeper who had very little else to give the Christchild.

You may think that you, too, have very little to offer, but it could be just the thing that someone else needs. We were glad to have Mrs. Diver at our table on Sunday many years ago. Give some thought to sharing your family celebration this year.

7

A Time for Friends

POST OFFICE

"I count myself in nothing else so happy
As in a soul remembering my good friends."

Shakespeare

t is at Christmastime that our friendships get their annual checkup, their yearly maintenance, and a megadose of nurturing to carry them through to another year. We know we should write regularly to our out-of-town friends and fully intend to get together with those who live close by, but the fact remains that most of us are doing pretty well if we make contact just once a year—at Christmas.

We might criticize this behavior and say, "Don't you think it's quite telling to give so much attention to friendships at Christmas only, when the media are there to remind you? Can't you remember unless someone tells you? Is guilt your motivator? Do you really like these people? Really? Oh, yeah? I don't believe you!"

The indictment seems fair. But since I am one of those who writes to most of her friends only once a year (yes, at Christmas), and since I inevitably do as much entertaining and party-going during the month of December as I do in the other eleven months combined (sue me!), and since it rarely occurs to me to give a good friend a small gift at any time other than at Christmas (do you?), I am strongly motivated to defend the yearly friendship catch-up that occurs at Christmas.

So let's be practical. While we know that we *should* give more thought to friendships during the rest of the year, let's concentrate on Christmas because it's the subject at hand. What can be done to celebrate Christmas with our friends, share our joy, and reinforce our relationship? Our efforts are generally directed to three areas: gift-giving, card-sending, and party-going.

The Big Swap

In their excellent book *Unplug the Christmas Machine,* Jo Robinson and Jean Coppock Staeheli present "The Self-Defeating Gift-Giving Rules" that our society employs to give order to our complicated relationships. They are:

1. Give a gift to someone you expect to get one from.

2. If someone gives you a gift unexpectedly, you should reciprocate that year, even if you had no previous intention of giving that person a present. (Some people have wrapped gifts set aside for just such an occasion.)

3. When you give someone a gift, you should plan to give that person a gift every year thereafter.

4. The amount of time and money you spend on a gift should be directly proportional to how much you care about the recipient.

5. The gift that you give someone should be equal in monetary value and/or personal significance to the one you receive from that person.

6. The presents you give someone should be fairly consistent over the years.

7. If you give a gift to a person in one category (for example: co-workers or neighbors), you should give gifts to everyone in that category. And these gifts should be similar.

8. The gifts you give your children should be equal in number and monetary value, while at the same time suiting the unique qualities of each child.

9. Men should *not* give gifts to their male friends, unless the gifts are alcoholic beverages. Women, however, are encouraged to give gifts to their female friends, and these gifts should *not* be alcohol.

10. Homemade gifts are more "meaningful" than store-bought ones. (*Unplug the Christmas Machine*, p. 105)

Does that ring a bell?
As much as we hate to admit it, we all follow these rules to

some extent. After buying presents for our children, we assess the amount of money spent on each and buy an extra toy or two for the daughter who was "shorted" because her brother got such an expensive piece of sports equipment (thereby keeping Rule #8).

Office gift exchanges, in which employees draw names of co-workers from a hat, are almost always accompanied with a monetary proviso like, "No more than five dollars" (see Rule #5). The busy executive can be seen at the department store cosmetic counter on his lunch hour, trying to find one all-purpose gift that will be appreciated by all the women in his office he is expected to give gifts to (Rule #7) because they always give him something (Rule #1) and he does this every year (Rule #3).

How else can we explain the mad dash for last-minute presents to give to those we unexpectedly received something from this year (Rule #2) or the faithful maintenance of gift lists from one year to the next so we can remember what we have given before—in hopes of getting some clue as to what we should give now (Rule #6)?

And our special friends and dearest loved ones will likely get from us a handmade present—something "From The Kitchen Of . . ." or a handcraft project that's been keeping us up until 1:00 A.M. every night for a month. Is there another way to show that person how much she means to us? (We adhere to Rules #4 and #10.) Men do tend to stay clear of all the fuss and bother, quietly footing the bill for The Big Swap. And one week before Christmas they make their annual trek to the liquor store and get gift-boxed bottles of premium brands for their business associates and best buddies (Rule #9).

We follow the rules because they promise order amidst chaos. Although they tend to thwart our spontaneity and can even threaten our happiness (not to mention bank balance), if everyone does what they are *supposed* to do, there will be few hurt feelings and general contentment all around when the paper is torn from the box.

There are some exceptions. Consider the plight of Art Buchwald and his wife who met a nice couple—Mr. and Mrs. Irving Hoffman—on a boat and decided to send them a Christmas card.

The Hoffmans in turn sent them a souvenir letter opener from St. Moritz and the race was on . . :

. . . When the next Christmas came around, my wife, who keeps the accounts in our house, said, "We have to get the Hoffmans a gift. They sent us a letter opener last year."

I protested that it wasn't necessary and that another Christmas card, perhaps with more elaborate printing, would suffice. But she was adamant. And so she went out and bought a paperweight, which she promptly dispatched with the season's greetings.

The day before Christmas a special delivery package arrived which contained four bottles of Scotch. It was too late to retaliate and my wife's Christmas was spoiled, thinking what the Hoffmans were thinking about us for sending them a lousy paperweight.

The next Christmas I went out and bought them a record album of Beethoven's nine symphonies, which set me back fifty dollars, but gave my wife her pride back.

The Hoffmans, who must have had some inkling of what I was up to, sent us a television set. Another Christmas was spoiled.

Fortunately we didn't have to wait for Christmas to get even. We were invited to the wedding of one of the Hoffman daughters and we sent as a gift a silver service from Cartier's.

We were feeling pretty good for a few months, but when my anniversary came around in October, I received a complete works of the Encyclopedia Americana in leather bindings.

These people were playing for real.

The next Christmas I bought them a small Van Gogh etching for one thousand dollars and gloated, but not for long. They sent us a set of Louis XIV chairs.

I was all for calling a truce, but my wife insisted I had to go on, even if it meant cutting down on gifts for the children.

"His birthday is in February," she said, "and yours doesn't come up until October. We'll have six months of peace."

I bought him a Vespa scooter for his birthday and delivered it myself just to see him eat his heart out.

It was a blow below the belt, but he recovered fast. Somehow he wheedled out of my wife that my son would be four years old in April.

When April came Hoffman sent ten shares of American Tel and Tel stock as a gift for the boy.

The gift exchanging went back and forth for the next few years without let-up. Feelings were so bitter that we didn't even talk to each other and did all our gift-giving by mail.

This Christmas I decided to fix Hoffman once and for all. I was going to give him a Thunderbird.

But while I was down at the dealer's looking them over, I got a call from my wife.

"Hold off," she cried excitedly. "All we got from the Hoffmans this year was a Christmas card."

"It's just a diversion," I said. "He's going to spring something on us Christmas Eve."

"I don't think so. It was a very cheap card and it had no return address."

"You really think they've given up?" I asked.

"I'm sure of it," my wife said.

"Why, that no good yellowbelly," I chortled. "He lost his nerve. I've got a good mind to send him the Thunderbird anyway."

"Oh, please don't," my wife begged. "He's probably suffering enough as it is, and it is Christmas."

"Okay," I said. "I'll let him off this time, but he better not start up with us again." (*Up the Seine and Down the Potomac with Art Buchwald*, pp. 118, 119.)

You say you don't like the rules? You're tired of paying homage to the reciprocity principle?

Like the Hoffmans, it will be up to you to make the first move. You could be viewed with suspicion. Your motivation will be questioned. But you might also experience a sensation not unlike losing sixty pounds, or making the last payment on a forty-eight-installment auto loan.

Begin by articulating the rules that you and your family (or family member) have been following, the ones you would like to breach. Explain to yourself and to your friend why you want to change, and then suggest an alternative. For example:

"Kids, in the past your father and I have been very careful to give each of you presents that were equal in number and value.

Sometimes it was hard, as when Josh needed a bike to get to school and we had to buy all three of you ten-speeds in order to keep everything even. We see now that that's not fair to us, and doesn't do you much good either. You know that you are all very special to us, and we'd rather have the gifts we give to you reflect your uniqueness instead of our insecurity. We'll be paying less attention to how much we spend from now on, and more attention to what you need and want."

Or this:

"Anne, it seems to me that we're caught in a bit of a gift trap. We started out giving each other little remembrances several years go, and now it's grown to the point that I think we're both becoming burdened with the cost and effort that our exchange brings. Would you like to go back to the little token gifts we used to give?"

You could explain it in a letter: "Dear Friends: Over the years Gladys and I have enjoyed exchanging gifts with you. Our home is graced with the many lovely items you've given us, and our souls (not to mention our bodies!) have been nourished by your kindness. We've enjoyed planning what we would give you, and looked forward with anticipation to what we would receive.

"But now our house is getting full, and our waistlines are filling out as well. We see that the time and effort and money we've been spending on gifts to our friends might be better placed with _____ (pick one: United Way, a world relief organization, UNICEF, any worthwhile cause). We have decided that they will be the recipient of our gifts this year. We want you to know that this decision in no way diminishes our love for you, but is instead our way of thanking you for all that you've meant to us in the past and will mean to us in the future by sharing with the less fortunate in our community (world). If you feel the way we do, we hope you'll consider giving our gift to someone else who needs it more than we do. Merry Christmas, and may God bestow his richest blessings on you all."

Communicating with your friends about the state of your gift-giving is part of the job of reconciling expectation (theirs and yours) with reality (a revised reality, in this case). If you don't do something to modify expectation, then reality will be a big disappointment. But if you revise the expectation that both of you have, you can live with the revised reality that will naturally follow.

What if you *like* to exchange gifts with your friends—nice gifts, homemade gifts? What if you endorse the reciprocity principle?

If you are fairly certain that your friend receives the same satisfaction from the exchange that you do, naturally you should continue the custom. The simple or "alternate" Christmas celebration isn't for everyone, or even most.

Relationships, though, are dynamic; they change over time. Even if you're content now, store away for future reference the assurance that if the custom ever does become cumbersome, you have it within your power to suggest modifications and bring about change.

There have been occasions on which I wanted to give a present to a friend, but balked at doing so because I thought it would set a precedent for our relationship that would be difficult to honor in the future. For example, I see an old Premium Saltines tin at a garage sale that I know Lynda would like. I picture it filled with cookies and given to my friend the following Christmas, but nix the idea of buying it because she might then feel obligated to get something for me, and I'd rather not initiate a yearly exchange.

I now think that the times I didn't buy the Premium Saltines tins were a mistake. It's a shame to deny ourselves and our friends expressions of spontaneous affection just because we suspect that it might get out of hand at some later date. We can prevent absurdity. I could have (should have) given her the gift and said, "I know we don't exchange Christmas gifts, and I don't necessarily want to start now, but when I saw this tin I couldn't pass it up. I hope you like it!"

If the gift is reciprocated (your friend plays by Rules #2, #3, and #5) against your will, then the ball is back in your court for the next year. Don't give a present, and you usually won't receive one. If your friend takes the initiative and gives a gift to you first, then you decide if you want to exchange gifts from now on (a legitimate decision), or if you want to stop (equally valid). If you want to stop, simply thank your friend and do nothing more.

If you want to break free of the "Ten Self-Defeating Gift-Giving Rules," then adopt this philosophy: "All Christmas giving should express love and goodwill." After that one rule has been kept, you are free to write your own laws and bylaws as to how you will conduct your gift-giving. You will be free to give token gifts or make major purchases for your friends; to keep a tradition of yearly gifts, or give only if and when you find an especially appropriate gift; to receive an extravagant gift without reciprocating, and to give an expensive gift without expecting one in return; to knock yourself out on a homemade gift, or to pick up some simple thing at the store; to spend more time, effort, thought, and money on gifts for others, or to do away with gift-giving altogether.

If your present is an expression of love and goodwill—not only for your special friend, but for your Creator and his creation—you will have great latitude in the conducting of your Christmas exchanges.

I can't help but think of the many laws of Israel that were summarized by Christ when he said that the most important commandments are to love God with all your heart, soul, and strength, and to love your neighbor as yourself. Once these commandments are obeyed, the others tend to take care of themselves.

And if your relationship with your friends (and consequently the gifts you give to them) reflect a love for God and a love for them, you won't go far wrong in what you do. If your intentions are good, your actions thoughtful, there is little chance that you will be misunderstood by those to whom you want to show special concern at Christmas.

From Our House to Your House

It seems that every time the price of a first-class stamp goes up, another segment of the population abandons the ritual of sending yearly Christmas greetings. (Erma Bombeck maintains that with the new rate hikes you meet a much better class of people at the Post

Office these days.) They tally the cost of cards, photo enclosures, duplicated letters, commemorative stamps and sealing wax and decide that cards aren't important.

And then there are the disgruntled receivers. They get a big, heavy card, enclosed in an embossed, foil-lined envelope, from their dear friends who moved to New Mexico four years ago, and open it expectantly to find that the beautiful card is beautifully imprinted

The Dr. Oliver Stanwoods

and figure that if *that's* all the Stanwoods think of them ("I don't care *how* much money they have, she could still have written a little note—after all!") then there's no point in continuing the charade any longer.

Still others dread the prospect of opening yet another card portraying that tipsy little Franciscan monk or a lewd Santa Claus doing the cancan with seven Las Vegas showgirls in reindeer costumes, each wishing a "Merry Shrishmas an' Habby Noooo Year!," wondering what ever happened to "Peace on Earth, Goodwill Toward Men."

If that weren't enough, there is a deluge of Christmas letters on poinsettia-bordered paper: "This year has been a wonderful one for Roger and me and the kids. As you know, Rog, Jr. won the Olympic gold medal in speed skating and the Decathlon. We're all so proud of him. Little Wendy is now the youngest student ever to graduate Validictorius from Harvard Law School. Roger has been made Emperor of his company, and I'm keeping busy with my new responsibilities as a United States Senator."

Is there anyone brave enough to write a Christmas letter that tells what *really* happened this past year? Apparently not, proclaim the veterans of decades of such letters. They cope with such nonsense by either responding in kind (spinning wild yarns about imaginary accomplishments or at least richly embellishing a meager reality), or refusing to play the game (hoping that lack of reply to such letters will eventually get them kicked off the offensive mailing list).

Well, it's not as bad as all that. Most of us truly enjoy almost every Christmas card we receive and do our best to get out some sort of greeting if we can. One Christmas Steve and I received a Christmas letter from some good friends, and it got me rethinking the whole subject of Christmas greetings. It started out predictably enough: a white envelope that held a photo greeting card and a triple-folded, mimeographed letter. We looked at the picture eagerly, since we hadn't seen our friends for years and they had two children we'd never set eyes on. We wanted to know how they looked these days. Very important. Then we read the letter. It began:

> For those of you tired of hearing from friends who just got promotions, are going to the Bahamas for a Christmas surprise, or whose children were nominated for the Nobel Prize in chemistry, our news will come as a welcome change. On the whole, 1983 was rough sledding for us, and we are rather relieved it's over.
>
> Our sense of misery began in January when we arrived in California . . .

The letter proceeded to describe the frustrations of finding an affordable home on the West Coast, an influx of friends who visited nonstop throughout the year, welcoming another child into the family via cesarean birth, and a parasitic illness that hit every family member. The sign-off was:

> Now you know why we never wrote you this year. We hope to do somewhat better in 1984. . . . Despite all, the year has been one of accomplishing just what we hoped for. As God leads us, we hope to build on a strong foundation.

I'd be lying if I said we didn't read the letter with some sadness. These were our friends, and they were having a bad time of it. Their letter brought back memories of our own disappointing childbirth experiences, adjustments (that word is too mild) with our second child, and the task of finding an adequate house that we could afford.

Yet we knew that the letter was honest. We knew that our relationship with these people still had substance, because they were willing to share these difficulties with us. We also felt a little guilty about the Christmas letter we had already dispatched to our friends, recalling that we mentioned only the good times of the past year and weren't brave enough—actually we didn't even consider it—to share our bad times as well.

Is anyone willing to send a Christmas greeting that reflects his deepest values, that communicates something of the essence of his life, that doesn't rely on a huge outlay of funds alone to convey its message? Is anyone willing to remember the purpose of sending Christmas cards, and to examine his own practices carefully to determine if they are fulfilling that purpose?

For some the answer may be to quit buying ready-made cards and design something that is more personal. As one who generally opts for the latter, I can say it's not the only answer. Homemade cards, no matter how simple they start out, have a way of turning into a Major Production and take a great deal of creativity, planning, and ability to execute. And there are always hitches: paint that runs, printers who are late (or you're late to the printers), envelopes that don't quite fit the card. Sometimes it seems to me that the time and effort I put into making cards might be better spent appending personal messages to American Greetings' best efforts.

Are you ready to put some thought into your cards, to try something different, to take a risk? One or more of the following suggestions might give you an idea:

1. Ready-made cards can often be purchased half-price a week or so before Christmas, and even cheaper after Christmas. Buy for next year.

2. The lull betwen Christmas and New Year's might be a good time to work on cards. By mailing cards late, you can correspond personally and intelligently to those who have already sent their cards.

3. Some people make a family tradition of addressing envelopes after Thanksgiving dinner or while watching football games during that long weekend. Addressing takes a lot of time and is something that can easily be done in advance. Let everybody get into the act.

4. Greet in-town friends that you see often in person or with a phone call, and save your card-sending money and efforts for those who live far away and that you don't see regularly.

5. Christmas postcards are attractive, and the price of mailing them is much less than a card-and-envelope greeting that requires first-class postage. You can buy these or make your own. (Check with the Post Office for size and weight regulations.)

6. Attractive cards can be purchased through charities like UNI-CEF, conservation groups like the National Wildlife Federation, Greenpeace, or the Audbon Society, or local civic groups and neighborhood associations. These organizations use the proceeds of card sales to help fund their activities. The cards are typically of very high quality, and in addition to sending a seasonal greeting convey a message of concern to the recipient. (The appendix contains addresses of some organizations that offer cards.)

7. Old Christmas cards can be recycled. Cut out the frontpiece art and, if you like, the inside message. Remount on card stock (obtained from a stationer) and send out again. This is an excellent project for grade-school-age children who like to cut and paste. You may wish to include on the back of the card a printed message explaining that the card is being recycled as an effort to exercise good stewardship over the world's resources, and that the money saved by doing so will be donated to a charity or group that is also working in that direction.

8. The town of Bethlehem, Connecticut, will help you give your cards a special touch. Every year their Post Office designs a rubber stamp with a Christmas greeting that graces every card, letter, and package that passes through their town. *Your* mail can pass through their town, no matter where you live.

Address and stamp your envelopes with the proper postage, and then package them up and send them to:

The Postmaster
Bethlehem, CT 06751

Enclose a note requesting that they be stamped with this year's seal and mailed from Bethlehem. They will be glad to do it, and your friends will be delighted too.

9. I have a friend who does not send Christmas cards. She collects the many cards she and her husband receive in a basket. Then, throughout the year, as they have their daily devotions after breakfast, they draw one card from the basket and pray specifically for the person or family who sent the card. Later in the day she follows up by sending a little preprinted letter explaining what happened, writing a personal note at the bottom. I look forward to receiving my card from Vivian, wondering when my name will be drawn.

10. "Christmas" cards may be sent out Valentine's Day, May Day, Independence Day, or whenever you think you'll have time to give the project the attention it deserves. New Year's cards are becoming popular with those who can't mobilize for Christmas, but there's no reason why you shouldn't send your yearly greeting whenever you like.

11. Your children may produce some work of art that you'd like to share with your friends. Take the masterpiece to the printer and discuss ways of duplicating it for cards. If your child is very prolific and ambitious, she could hand-decorate each card with an original drawing.

12. Mount duplicates of a favorite snapshot on a piece of 8½ x 11 paper (maybe colored) that has been French-folded. The inside of the card features the message you want to send. The card can also open up to reveal a letter that has been printed on the inside. This idea incorporates a photo, a greeting, and a letter—just about everything you'd want to send. It's our family favorite.

13. Boutiques, art galleries, Third-World shops, and other locally-owned businesses in your area may carry handmade and specialty cards that reflect your tastes and interests, and those of the community you live in.

14. Open cards as a family at the dinner table. If you receive many cards, let each member of the family draw one from a basket where they are accumulating, open it, and read it to the rest of the family. Take some time to talk about the person who sent it, telling those who don't know that person something about him: how you met, where he lives, what is special about him.

15. Display cards by clipping them onto a cord that is draped across a wall, over a doorway, or down a door jamb; place them on a mantel or windowsill; tape them to windowpanes; decorate a buffet table with standing cards; keep them in a tray or basket on the coffee table so they can be enjoyed by guests. A great deal of expense and thought has gone into those cards. Make the most of it!

You may have the idea that the traditional Christmas greeting has gotten way out of hand, and that there's no hope for redeeming it. But that's simply not true. My attitude was changed by just one honest Christmas letter, and that same letter must surely have encouraged other people to evaluate their greetings too.

Even if you're not up to a radical departure from what you've always done, you can make some changes—*slight* changes. And it's very possible that your friends, who view the fruits of your effort, will respond in kind.

The Christmas Party

We restore and nourish friendships by formal and informal get-togethers—parties. For most people, the Christmas season is full of opportunities to socialize. We entertain and are entertained at parties. There are three main kinds of parties that we'll talk about here.*

The Office Party

How would magazines have any cartoons with which to fill their pages during the month of December if not for The Office Party? The very words conjure up images of overweight executives teetering drunkenly on their desks while shapely secretaries stave off the advances of shipping clerks by the water cooler.

In recent years, the Christmas-Eve-3:00-Friday-Afternoon party has declined in popularity, and we can only applaud its demise. Such celebrations take parents away from their families and encourage the kind of revelry that makes it hard to return to work with dignity on the 26th.

More popular now are small luncheons organized by co-workers (sometimes with a gift exchange), all-company parties held at nice hotels or banquet facilities with spouses invited and entertainment provided, dinner parties given by the boss for employees and their families in his or her home, or simply Christmas bonuses in lieu of an expensive party. Each of these options is, to my mind, an improvement over the no-spouse-allowed affairs.

Why have an office party at all? The purpose of a party is threefold:

To reward workers for service. This can be traced to the British custom of Boxing Day (December 26) when employers give employees an end-of-the-year bonus to thank them for their loyalty and hard work on behalf of the company.

To provide an opportunity for employees on different rungs of the corporate ladder to socialize, thereby creating a sense of sympathy and goodwill between workers that will encourage higher productivity and greater job satisfaction. (Well, one does feel a bit differently about the payroll supervisor once one has seen her do

---

*See Chapter 5 for directions on how to have a Birthday Party for Jesus; Chapter 6 for hints on how to have a successful Family Reunion; Chapter 8 for a discussion of neighborhood get-togethers; Chapter 9 for church-related activities.

the bugaloo with the personnel manager. The president seems more of a regular guy once you've met his wife. It turns out that the fellow two stations down on the assembly line likes bass fishing too—you found this out over dinner—and now you like him better.) Employers want employees to form personal relationships with co-workers and supervisors that will contribute to positive feelings about the company.

To spend money. "Not at *my* company," you say. Although it isn't the biggest concern in many cases, Christmas parties (and end-of-the-year bonuses) are often planned with the purpose of putting money into celebration (and employees' pockets) before the IRS has a chance to tax it. So the Christmas party is often a carefully calculated (and enjoyable) way of avoiding taxation.

Does your company party accomplish this purpose? If the point is just to spend money before the end of the year, that's quite easy to manage. But is it a true reward for faithful workers? Does it give employees a chance to scale the walls separating management and labor so they can understand and appreciate one another better?

In recent years newspapers have carried stories of workers who opted to forego their annual party, asking instead that their employer donate the money that would have been used for it to Boys Clubs, American Cancer Society, or some other cause. Others have foregone their traditional three-hour-lunch on Christmas Eve Day and used the money they saved for some worthwhile purpose. Many businesses sponsor "Toys for Tots" drives. In our town, if you have cable TV hooked up during the month of December, Cablevision will donate $15 to the Neediest Kids Fund.

In nearly every case, when companies have decided to direct their energies toward charity instead of their own celebration, it's been at the request of the employees. It is the workers who must send the message to management that they are willing to give up something of their own (a Christmas party) and give it to someone whose need is greater.

Many times we feel that our individual efforts are insufficient to make a difference when we tackle the problems of the world. When we join with our employer and fellow employees, however, we have greater resources at our disposal, and can join our efforts with those of others to make the holidays brighter for someone in need.

The Perfunctory Party

"Okay, let's see now. I think we can pretty much take care of everybody if we cut out dinner, and just serve hot hors d'oveures and cocktails. That's twenty-three couples and eight singles for a total of fifty-four—if they all come, which they won't—that we can handle in just one evening. It'll cost a lot, but at least we can get all those people paid back, and it's a lot easier than having a bunch of smaller dinner parties. Oh, yeah, we might as well include my boss while we're at it. He won't know anybody, but, oh well . . . if he doesn't want to come that's up to him. At least I invited him."

Ever suspect that you've been a guest at a party like that? Is that the way you do your parties? It's too bad when something that should be an expression of hospitality and friendship mutates into a means of repaying entertaining debts to asociates you "owe" because they entertained you once.

Wives (and more recently husbands) of business executives and spouses of people who routinely mix business and pleasure are often found attending or hosting parties whose primary purpose is to repay professional favors, ease the way for business deals, or impress potential clients. They often tire of putting on their best face and displaying their best manners for people they haven't met and probably don't care for, all the while pretending that there's no place they'd rather be.

The Perfunctory Party—who needs it? You may need it. At some time in our lives, most of us find ourselves in a position where we must at least attempt to make a party given merely to repay social debts or insure business success look like a warm gathering of dear and loving friends.

As it relates to Christmas, the first question to ask yourself when in this situation is, "Is now the time?" In asking this question, we assume that you are busy, the people on your guest list are busy, and it's possible that another time of the year might be better in terms of the availability of guests and your ability to execute the party successfully. Of course, if you are the invited there's not much you can do about a host who decides to even the score on entertaining before the end of the calendar year. But if you are the host, you can consider alternative times. The December issues of women's magazines, radio and TV advertisements, television programming, and department store displays are there to remind you that you have several unreciprocated dinner parties outstanding and that you need to get around to doing something about it. Hold that thought! Accept the reminder and mark something on your calendar in January or February; plan to do your entertaining then, when there is less competition for time and effort.

The second question to ask is, "Can this party be bumped up a notch in terms of meaning and fellowship?" This question should be asked by both host and guest. Is there anything you can do to make your gathering more enjoyable and less perfunctory or obligatory?

As a host, you might take a second look at the guest list and modify it so that people you believe would have similar interests will be included and those who are likely to detract from the good time are invited to some other function at which they'll be more comfortable. Don't doom your party to failure by inviting people whom you know will dislike being with each other.

You could also plan activities that are a little different than what is expected. How about including these people's children? While family parties are very common for some of us (those of us who have trouble getting sitters!), there are some people who rarely do anything socially with their families. They might appreciate such an "innovation." Instead of cocktails and appetizers, how about a Saturday morning brunch, or a Sunday evening build-your-own-pizza party? It takes a little nerve to deviate from what you know to be the expected manner of entertaining, but remember that if it is expected, it's also been done so many times before that people are likely getting tired of it. It's highly probable that your attempt to mix things up a little bit, even though not perfectly executed, will be greatly appreciated.

When you are invited to what you suspect is a Perfunctory Party, leave your cynicism at home. Social gatherings have a way of living up to their guest's expectations. When a guest arrives at the door believing that he'll be bored and uncomfortable, he's rarely disappointed. But when he accepts the invitation with gratitude, anticipates the event with enthusiasm, and attends with optimism, the least-promising of parties begins to exhibit possibilities.

The Best-of-Friends Party

And why not save the best until last? After the Acme Flange and Fawcet Company Christmas banquet is over, after the pay-'em-back party is over, it's time to get together with the people we really like, and enjoy each other's company in the spirit of Christmas. Under this heading we include every and all social occasions spent with the people we consider our friends.

As with The Perfunctory Party, when it comes to socializing with your friends it is a good idea to consider whether or not Christmas is the best time to do so. Even the most eagerly anticipated events become an imposition when they take place on the evening after the school Christmas pageant, or are the fifth party in a week, or require clothing that you can't afford to rent (let alone buy) or elaborate and exhausting preparations at what is already the busiest time of the year.

So you can ask, "Is now the time?" If friends are coming from out-of-town for the holidays, if the party is an important tradition you don't want to give up, if the theme of your party revolves around Christmas specifically (caroling, for example), if you have the time and your friends have the time, the answer is "yes."

If you could get together at any other time of the year, and would just as soon do so, the answer might be "no." When we lived in Chicago, we worked with a great bunch of people who loved to get together socially. I doubt if a week went by that we didn't have something planned with the people we worked with. As I look back on that time, I see that we might have all done ourselves a favor by calling a moratorium on our socializing during the Christmas season, reserving our time and energies for those activities that couldn't possibly take place at any other time. As it was, we proceeded full-throttle through the month of December with our regular regimen of parties, dinners, and outings. Those were the days when Christmas Day found me overfed, overentertained, and overtired.

If you will be gathering with friends over the holidays—or any time—cash in on the fact that good friends will understand if all the china doesn't match or you need help in the kitchen. Friends understand why you had to be late or need to leave early. You have ample opportunity to be prim and proper when you're with "strangers"; so celebrate the fact that you can let your hair down with your friends.

The following party ideas work well at a Best-of-Friends Party:

—Ask guests to bring a big batch of their favorite cookies or Christmas candy. After eating to your heart's content, exchange the leftovers so everyone goes home with a plate of assorted goodies.

—Spend your time together working on a project that will benefit someone else: bake for an elderly shut-in, wrap presents for needy children, assemble the church newsletter.

—Pick out a charity that you like (orphanage, family shelter, etc.) and contact them, asking them what their needs are for the work they do. Having done your research, issue invitations to your friends that include a gift list from which they can pick one or more items to bring to the party. Part of the fun is showing each other what you're giving (go on—get competitive and try to outdo each other!) and then wrapping it up.

—Get together to work on Christmas crafts. Make potato block print wrapping paper or Christmas cards; tie a quilt; sew doll clothes; fashion Christmas tree ornaments; assemble pine cone wreaths.

—Ask your friends to bring their favorite Christmas record or tape and snapshots of their past Christmases.

—Have a tree trimming party.

—Include children, and focus your activity on a Birthday Party for Jesus.

—Ask each guest to bring someone to the party that the other guests have not met before.

—Play board games a la "musical chairs." Set a timer to ring every thirty minutes, at which time everyone changes places. The game goes on continuously with new players, and it doesn't really matter who "wins."

—Ask each person to bring a soup ingredient, and use all the donated items to make "stone soup." (You could have the stock already boiling and ready to go since that takes awhile.)

—Dress up—a novel idea if most of your entertaining is informal. Send invitations that stipulate formal attire required; it could be fun!

—Ask your guests to come-as-they-were five, ten, twenty, or forty Christmases ago.

Entertaining—even entertaining good friends—often involves taking a risk. Few of us feel that we have a large enough apartment or house in which to entertain, or enough matching dishes, or that we are good enough cooks or gracious enough hosts to do the kind of entertaining we'd like to do.

But who does? If we decide that the purpose of socializing is to enjoy our friends, then the spectre of a fallen soufflé, a shortage of chairs, or an overflow of guests into the basement becomes less threatening, and a whole range of possibilities opens to us. The important factor is people. The beautiful pictures of fancy buffets in *Better Homes and Gardens* or *Family Circle* can't hold a candle to anything you do, because those pictures are for show, but your party is for people.

Don't worry about parties you've been to or—worse yet— parties you've seen on television shows or in liquor advertisements. They aren't real. You are real, and your friends are real. Don't take on more than you can handle, and don't be afraid to do your own thing. If you entertain and are entertained for the purpose of enjoying people, you won't go far wrong.

8

A Time for Community

hristmas is a time to look beyond ourselves, our families, and our friends and see those whose lives don't ordinarily intersect with our own. It is a time for those who have the light to let it shine; to share the hope within us with those around us; to witness in whatever way we can to the truth that was proclaimed through Christ's birth.

"Every year it gets worse," laments Vera. "First there was that big brouhaha about the nativity scene in front of the city offices building. So they took that down. Then the Board of Education decided that Christmas couldn't be celebrated as a religious holiday; so we couldn't talk to the children about Christ's birth or sing 'Silent Night' with the school children. It is *Christmas* after all! Then we had to start calling everything we did a holiday this-or-that, like the winter holiday instead of Christmas break, or holiday program, or holiday singing. Oh, it's gotten way out of hand. And every year it gets worse."

How does one celebrate Christmas in the community? The fact that we live in a pluralistic society, that our Constitution mandates separation of church and state, determines that what is essentially a religious holiday cannot be imposed on those who do not hold to that religious belief. Recent policies, legislation, and court decisions have made us aware that Christians might be barred from certain celebrative activities.

A few people are getting militant. They are lobbying school boards, filing suits in local and federal courts, and electing legislators who will represent and defend the majority (assumed to be traditionally Christian) point of view. They want a city to be able to have a paid-by-taxes nativity scene in front of the city hall, and they want public school children to sing religious carols in school.

The problem brings up all sorts of legal issues that can't be dealt with here. I would submit, though, that in organizing and participating in community festivals and celebrations, such observances should be employed as a means of witnessing to others about the joy of the Christian faith, rather than as a bludgeon to hit nonbelievers over the head. Consequently, when the personal religious celebration is expanded to the public observance, it should be done in such a way that it peacefully proclaims the Good News of the birth of Christ, rather than frantically screaming at those who have non-Christian beliefs.

From a purely strategic point of view, more good will come from letting the church promote the religious significance of Christmas than from forcing our secular society to incorporate Christian symbols into its celebration when it neither respects the symbols nor properly understands them.

Those who do not believe that the Son of God was born to a virgin, who do not believe that Christ's birth was the turning-point in humankind's history and relationship to God, who do not believe that that event has any significance for them personally—these people cannot be relied upon to conscientiously and responsibly present Christian symbols and theology.

It's up to each one of us to take the initiative and let our presence be felt in the community. We can start close to home.

On the Street Where You Live

The street where you live is also the apartment complex, suburb, or the dormitory in which you live. It encompasses those people who live near you—say, within walking distance—and who form your neighborhood community.

The arrival of the Christmas holiday brings a terrific excuse for getting to know your neighbors. Many of us live in apartments and have never met our next-door neighbors, even though they and we have been living side by side for years. And there is often no formal or accepted way of introducing ourselves and getting to know new families on the street.

Some people, apparently, feel threatened when their close neighbors take an interest in them. Most of us, though, recall a time when neighbors knew and cared for one another, and yearn for a place in a close-knit community. Recent years have seen a trend toward organizing neighborhood crime prevention programs, the rise of neighborhood, residents,' and tenants' associations, and even a revival of block parties. If we once coveted our privacy, we now seem ready to resume our involvement with our neighbors.

Christmas provides an opportunity for getting to know our neighbors. The person who goes door-to-door with fruitcake for her neighbors will be viewed as an embodiment of the spirit of Christmas by nearly everyone; if she did it at any other time of the year she would be viewed with unbridled suspicion. At what other time of the year can you sing to your neighbors, invite them over for a potluck supper, or string colored lights between your houses with so little ego risk?

Christmas is also a uniquely intergenerational holiday. It naturally places toddlers and the elderly together with little thought about the disparity of their ages. Families with small children might think they have little in common with four single college students who live next door or the retired couple across the street, but when Christmas comes around, they are one big family: parents and children, aunts and uncles, grandma and grandpa.

Here are some ideas to get you started in involving your neighbors in your Christmas celebration. Remember, don't try to do everything; it'll be too much. Pick one or two ideas that pique your interest and give it a try.

1. Invite neighbors for a cookie exchange. Each guest brings a large batch of cookies, and when everyone has eaten his fill, the leftovers are exchanged so each person goes home with an assortment. You provide the coffee, spiced cider, punch, eggnog, or whatever you'll be having to drink.

2. Have a Birthday Party for Jesus for the children on your block (see page 98 for details). This can be a strong Christian witness to your neighbors.

3. Organize a potluck supper, lunch, or—better yet—breakfast. If your group is going to be small and you are worried about a balanced menu, you can give food assignments, making them general so that each guest can exercise his own creativity. For example, stipulate, "Something with protein" as opposed to "Two twelve-ounce packages of brown-and-serve link sausage (pork)."

4. Go caroling. First, get your group of carolers. They might

be members of your church youth group, your Sunday School class, your softball team (that you haven't seen since August), your co-workers, your Bible study group. About a week before the event, drop a note in your neighbors' mailboxes telling them which night you'll be out, and asking them to put on their porch light if they'd like to be sung to. (This saves you the embarrasment of singing to a vacant home or apartment house balcony, and gives your neighbors a chance to have cookies ready for you.) You must have songsheets for each caroler and might consider having a brief practice at your place before you begin. Plan on returning to your house or apartment for refreshments when you're done.

5. In the fall (September or October, so everyone will have time to plan for it) approach your neighbors about the idea of coordinating Christmas decorations. If you have a traditional neighborhood—single-family houses along a street—you could:

—String colored lights on your eaves and between houses, connecting the entire block.

—Have everyone place candles (real or electric) in their windows—all the same, all lit every night for an agreed-upon period of time (say, December 16-26).

—Fill brown grocery bags with sand, and place a candle in each bag (held firmly by the sand). These bags can line the sidewalks of each home for a beautiful effect. Try six to eight bags on each side of each walkway. One neighbor might volunteer to go to a gravel-yard and pick up enough sand for everyone. When the holidays are over, the sand can be added to the kids' sandpile or saved for next year.

Do you live in an apartment? Slip a note under each tenant's door, asking if they would like to work on some coordinated decorations, suggesting that they meet in your apartment to discuss ideas. You could:

—Outline balconies with colored lights.

—Pool money to buy decorations for a fir tree (or any tree) outside your building; purchase an artificial tree for the lobby; get outdoor lighting for the building. The decorations would become the responsibility of whatever tenants live in the building at a given time, and could be used and added to over the years. In other words, a tenant who moves out doesn't take her share of decorations with her—they stay with the building.

—Does someone in your building know how to make wreaths out of pine cones, corn husks, grapevines, or calico? Spend an evening or two together making design-coordinated wreaths that each tenant can hang on her or his door. In addition to beautiful matching decorations, you will have an opportunity to get to know each other better as you slave over your masterpieces.

—Candles (real or electric) in every window of an apartment building have a stunning effect. Even a duplex or fourplex has a lot of windows. If you can get everyone in the building to cooperate, it will be spectacular.

6. Christmas is a difficult time for the elderly in your neighborhood or apartment building. Do you know who they are? Perhaps there is something you can do for them:

—Many of the elderly have given up on having a Christmas tree because they are unable to get out and buy one or can't assemble their artificial one. You could quite easily do either of these things for them.

—Get some neighbors together to help decorate your elderly friend's tree.

—Offer to do their holiday grocery shopping along with your own.

—Make a double batch of goodies—cookies, candy, bread—and give the extra away.

—Be sure your caroling party makes it to your elderly friend's home.

—Offer to take them to church with you on Christmas Eve or Christmas Day.

—Involve your children. They can read Christmas articles and books to the elderly, help with chores, recite a Christmas poem.

—Invite some elderly person on your block to spend Christmas Day with you, adopting them as an honorary grandparent. You needn't make a special fuss. In most cases, they'll be grateful to simply be there.

—Use your Christmas experience as a springboard to show caring the rest of the year.

Our Little Town

It is at the local level that questions are most often raised concerning the propriety of blending the religious and secular elements of Christmas. If we decide, though, that all celebrations will be carried out with the intent of *proclaiming* the Good News instead of *insisting* upon it, then we can initiate (as opposed to legislate) community observances, enlisting the aid and support of like-minded friends and neighbors.

There are undoubtedly celebrations in your own community that you can plug into right away. Churches, civic groups, businesses, and ad hoc committees of enthusiastic people organize all sorts of holiday activities, many of which you can wholeheartedly endorse.

In the city where I live, there are scores of interesting and worthwhile activities: a community *Messiah* sing; a bank that distributes dolls which have been beautifully dressed by volunteers and are then given to needy children through the Salvation Army; the Shriner Christmas party at the municipal auditorium, benefiting the handicapped; a day when a new toy will be accepted in lieu of the normal fare on the city transit system; radio stations that collect money and gift donations to provide Christmas toys for children; community centers that distribute food baskets for needy families; newspaper coverage of neighborhoods with especially nice outdoor lights and displays; Christmas decorations in the rotunda of the State Capitol building; department store Santas; and a host of other "come one, come all" events.

Your town is like mine, no matter how small or how large. In rural areas, pageants and festivals are often cooperative events involving many communities; in large cities, the opportunities are endless—more than any one person or family can take advantage of.

A Different Kind Of Celebration

The Alternate Celebrations Catalog is a good resource for those who want a radical departure from the usual community affairs. The authors state that many people "experience anger and frustration at having their emotions manipulated by the 'hard sell' to buy at Christmas." They suggest that "The will to be fair, to share, to live on less, to *practice* justice in our lifestyle and celebrations . . . this is where we can begin to incarnate our conviction that people can change the world" (pp. 86, 87).

How does one practice justice in celebrations? This is an especially relevant question when we broach the subject of how we should interact with our community during the Christmas season. First, we must have an inner resolve to conduct our lives in such a way that the poor and powerless are not exploited and destroyed by our actions. Second, we must organize with others of like mind to create a forum for our convictions that the community-at-large can attend and from which they can draw their own conclusions about their own celebrations.

Are you intrigued with the idea of a different kind of Christmas celebration in your community? One possibility is an "Alternate" Christmas Festival. It differs from a Main Street Parade or Community Tree Lighting in that its purpose is to provide information, ideas, and support for those who are responsive to the challenge to celebrate the birth of Christ in a more responsible way. The festival can include booths, displays, and information tables from social change groups, neighborhood associations, and religious organizations. Self-help craft groups can demonstrate, display, and sell their creations (some of the Third-World craft distributors listed in the appendix of this book will provide goods on consignment for such a festival). Food items can be sold, especially those that are made with an eye toward careful handling of the world's food supply: homemade bread, "natural" cookies, homemade pasta, locally grown produce. The Food Pantry or Hunger Task Force in your town might like to come to the festival with information about their activities, as would food co-ops and collective buying services.

Invite participants who have skills in creating handmade Christmas gifts. Local musicians can sing and play and organize dancing. A skilled songleader can get everyone singing.

Perhaps a book table could be set up, presenting publications and books that have relevance to the issue of an alternative Christmas celebration. A live tree could be decorated with handmade ornaments (the tree to be planted later). Santa Claus should be there, of course, but dressed in green instead of red to emphasize that at your festival you are exploring a different way of celebrating; you are considering alternatives.

The Alternate Celebrations Catalog (see publishing information in the bibliography) has more detailed information about organizing such a festival, as well as ideas about how other aspects of our celebrative existence can be changed to reflect more Christian and human values. It may or may not be something that you can adopt absolutely, but it will definitely get you thinking in other directions, especially when it comes to deciding how you will—or will not—plug into your community at Christmas.

Peace on Earth, Goodwill Toward Men

All over the world, in every country where the Christian message has been carried by pilgrims and missionaries, the faithful gather to celebrate the nativity of the Christchild. Our own country is blessed with the customs of many nations, brought to us by immigrants who gifted the New Land with their Old World traditions.

The Christmas tree from Germany, baked goods of all sorts from the Scandinavian countries, the crèche from Italy, the Victorian customs of England, St. Nicholas of Holland, *piñatas* of Mexico are all represented in our culture. Some customs are now thoroughly American, observed by nearly everyone in this country. Others are kept alive by those of our number who still have strong ties to the old country, wherever that may be.

The message of the angels, "Peace on Earth, Goodwill Toward Men," expresses the longing of our hearts: universal peace and worldwide understanding. In the past, it has been traditional for countries at war to observe a truce on Christmas Day. We have all heard accounts of Christmas Day truces during World War I, in which American and German soldiers came out of the trenches to share with each other their holiday rations and to set aside—if only for a day—the fighting and hatred. The idea that this can happen inspires hope that our leaders, too, will one day be ready to resolve their differences.

If we are aware of the common brotherhood of man during the Christmas season, if we have new hope for our ability to exist

peacefully with other nations, if we delight in the ri[...]
cultures' celebrative customs, we are also reminded tha[...] w[...]
a long way from true peace on earth and goodwill toward men.

Our Christmas preparations are interrupted by the evening
news, declaring that the droughts, terrorism, and oppression continue unabated; even declared truces have been broken by one or both
sides. Our abundant feasts are marred by the realization that over
one half of the world's population is still hungry, Christmas or not.
We know that there are young men and women in our armed forces
who are away from their families on Christmas Day, charged with
the impossible task of keeping peace and order in the world.

Still, it is worthwhile to find opportunities in our celebration
of Christmas to work toward justice. We must believe and assert
that one person can make a difference. For although the world gets
larger and more complex with its rising population and compound-
ed problems, it also gets smaller with each new advance in transpor-
tation and communication. Our great-grandparents wouldn't even
have heard about a drought in Ethiopia; these days, we know about
it immediately and can quickly send help to victims.

We can heighten our own consciousness and that of our
friends and families by looking to the world we live in for clues and
cues on how we might celebrate Christmas in a manner that recognizes the variety and predicaments of the world's people.

1. Include a different country's celebration in your own. You might
choose to have a holiday meal of a favorite cuisine, decorating the
table with crafts from that country. My mother-in-law does this.
Each year she works the Christmas dinner around an ethnic theme:
once it was Hawaiian, once Italian (lasagna instead of turkey—
terrific!), and I believe she's contemplating Mexican for next year.
For those who tire of "the same old thing," having something
different every year can be a tradition too!

2. At the bookstore or library, get books that chronicle holiday
customs around the world or fairy tales and stories from other
countries. Read a little every day—across the cleared dinner table
with your family, or before bed with your children. As you do so,

emphasize that each country's traditions and myths are different, all beautiful and wonderful in their own right.

3. Study one country during the Advent season, making it part of your Advent devotions. You might choose a country where your church has missionaries, that you have visited, that you have friends in, or that was the home of your ancestors. Learn as much as you can about its history and its current social and political situation. Pray about its problems, and do what you can do to help effect a change for its people. Send a money donation to missionaries there; write your elected officials about pending legislation or national policies that affect it; write a letter to the editor of your local newspaper expressing an opinion you have about that country.

4. In your Christmas buying, support organizations that are working toward world peace. You can get Christmas cards from UNICEF, books and food gifts from Koininia Farms, or shop locally at Third-World shops (see the appendix).

5. Consider the drain on the world economy that our typically wasteful consumption practices cause. When Americans—and others in the so-called "developed" countries—live high on the hog, others may pay the price. High levels of consumption by 30 percent of the world's population are directly related to the continued impoverishment of the other 70 percent. In 1982 we spent $20 billion dollars ($20,000,000,000!) on Christmas! This is a moral issue that we—as individuals—can address. Work toward world peace by conducting your life in an ecologically and economically responsible way.

6. Invite a foreign student or someone from another country to spend Christmas with you. Foreign students are sometimes "kicked out" when their dormitory housing shuts down over the Christmas holidays, and they have nowhere to go. Do you have a spare bedroom or a hide-a-bed in your living room? Christmas is a great time to give visitors a taste of what our American celebrations are like (interesting from a purely anthropological point of view) and to

learn about someone else's country. Ask your gu
would be able to cook a meal or native dish for you.

7. Many of us live near an ethnic community that celebrates its old-world customs. Big cities have ethnic neighborhoods whose restaurants, social clubs, civic groups, and churches provide opportunities for "outsiders" to join in on their authentic Christmas celebrations. Many small towns all across the country still capitalize on the fact that their population is largely composed of the descendants of early immigrants (like the Swedes of Lindsborg, Kansas), holding elaborate festivals, pageants, and celebrations that are the next best thing to being there.

8. "Peace is not a season; it is a way of life." Pray for and practice peace at Christmas, and throughout the year.

Drop a Dollar in the Kettle

Many of us plan, at Christmastime, to give some kind of special contribution to charity. In the midst of orchestrating our own celebration—be it lavish or simple—we are impressed with the needs of the world, our comparative wealth, and the multitude of worthy causes begging for our financial participation. Even when our own budget is suffering under the load of extra expenditures for food, clothing, entertainment, and presents, we find ourselves dropping coins into the Salvation Army bucket at the shopping center or answering a direct-mail appeal from our favorite charity.

We want to give at Christmas, not only to our family and friends, but also to the needy of our community and the world. And if our giving is more motivated by guilt than gratitude—well, it all goes to the same place anyway. No matter *why* the money is given, the fact remains that it can be put to good use by the people who organize these efforts, right?

Of course right. While the Lord may love a cheerful giver, the fact remains that currency has an intrinsic value that exists without reference to the attitude of its owner at the time it was turned over to the charity. So let's not worry any more about "tainted" money which, it has been noted, merely means that there " 'taint hardly ever enough."

But if we are committed to trying to reconcile our expectations with our reality, we will first admit that the expected joy and satisfaction that we hope will result from our generosity is not often met by the reality of our giving. Why is it that we can't get what we want when we give something away?

I would suggest that our dissatisfaction arises from two fallacies in our giving: we give for the wrong reason, and we give the wrong things.

First, we give for the wrong reason. Now I do not believe that unless a person can give something cheerfully, she shouldn't give at all. There are simply too many cheerless people and too much to be done in this world—work that requires substantial funding—for me to go along with this. I do not believe that money given grudgingly carries with it a curse that will invalidate its potential for good once it reaches its destination. I believe that $10 given reluctantly to CARE will buy as much rice for a hungry child as $10 given gleefully.

But when it comes to Christmas giving, the disparity between our wasteful, lavish celebration and the condition of the rest of the world's population hits home as it does few other times of the year. When we exhaustedly view the stacks of expensive cartoon-character and embossed-foil wrapping paper and shiny stick-on bows, used once and now ready to be burned in the fireplace; the battery-operated tin toys that will either be broken in ten days or chucked, all-but-forgotten, into an overcrowded toy box; the tasted but uneaten food that will be thrown down the garbage disposal; the extra money spent to fill dubious needs with luxuries—ivory toothpicks, perfumed soap-on-a-rope, Moroccan leather bookmarks, a gold-plated corkscrew; the pile of ridiculous "joke gifts"—pet rocks and so forth—then it's hard not to feel a twinge of guilt at all the waste and all the pointless extravagance.

So our holiday giving is more often than not a buy-out. We send money to missions so we can have our holiday in peace. Is it any wonder that we don't get the satisfaction we want? For no matter how much we give away, we must still deal [ ] kept, and what we did with what we kept.

We might bridge the gap between expectation and reality more effectively if we would pay closer attention to our own spending, not necessarily for reasons of thrift—although that's worth considering—but as an attempt to live a responsible existence in this world, aware of the drain we put on the world's resources, and mindful of our interrelatedness with the rest of the world's peoples.

Secondly, we give the wrong things. This isn't always our fault. Some charities and organizations are asking for the wrong things, and we can't assume all the blame for giving them what they say they need.

Armand Marquiset, the French artistocrat who founded the Little Brothers of the Poor, was once a carefree young man who traveled the world in search of excitement and adventure. At the age of thirty, after the death of his grandmother, he devoted his life to the service of the poor, eventually forfeiting his entire fortune for their care, especially the care of the elderly.

He coined a phrase that has now become famous—"Flowers Before Bread"—beause he believed that all people, rich and poor, are worthy of respect and dignity. He was much criticized for giving the poor holiday food baskets containing smoked oysters and caviar, providing summer vacations in castles, or giving diamonds to couples who had been married sixty years. Some donors were offended by his extravagance, calling him "Armand the Magnific."

But a well-dressed lady who reproached him for having given too lavishly to the elderly received this reply: "Madam, there are many people who will be very embarrassed when they arrive in Paradise and see on our Lord the castoffs that they have given to the poor."

Marquiset visited Mother Theresa in India, laying red roses at the foot of each bed where men in misery lay dying. He later told Pope Paul VI, "Never did I feel a stronger feeling that each of them had become Christ for me," to which the Pope replied, "Each of them *was* Christ."

Can we take too literally Christ's words that "whatever is done unto the least of these my brethren is done unto me"? I think not.

While there is certainly a place for the giving of our castoffs to Goodwill Industries or the Junior League Thrift Store, there is, as Doris Jantzen Longacre pointed out in *Living More With Less*, much more to be said for having very little to give such organizations because we have been careful in our purchasing and frugal in the use of our possessions.

We give the wrong things. We give what is left over, we give what doesn't fit, we give what is worn out, we give what is broken. We proudly deposit a baby doll whose hair has been shorn and whose body is covered with crayon marks into a large bin in the shopping mall—a converted trash can marked "Christmas for Kids"—and wonder why we don't feel better about our donation. If we have a dollar or two left over after all our Christmas shopping has been done, and we have had lunch at the department store tearoom, and we have picked up some candy for our kids, and we have figured out how much parking will cost—*then* we'll drop a buck in the Salvation Army bucket. We find that we are unable to get even one more item of clothing into our overstuffed walk-in closets; so we piously clean out the mess, throwing outdated, stained, and shabby clothing into a large bag given to us by the Disabled American Veterans. Whew! We've killed three birds with one stone: cleaned out the closet, helped the vets, and gotten a great end-of-the-year tax deduction.

Is it any wonder we are unsatisfied with our benevolence? Are we willing to see the face of Christ on each shopper at the Goodwill store, on each poor child who will receive a doll through the "Christmas for Kids" program, on each "bum" who walks through the food line at the Salvation Army on Christmas Day?

If so, we will give for different reasons, and we will give different things. We will give to charity out of charity, out of love. We will give because we recognize our kinship with the poor of the world. We will alter our own lifestyles so that we are living more responsibly. And we won't give away only what we don't want or what is left over. We will give away the best; we will give away the first. We will give Flowers Before Bread.

The appendix contains addresses and information about chari-

table and relief organizations that you might want t
porting. On a more general level, you can challenge
following ways.

1. Let presents to friends and relatives do double-duty. You can give a nice gift to a friend that also supports an organization and people who are working toward self-support. There are organizations employing indigenous people making their native crafts in this country. The Koinonia farms grow pecans and peanuts and make wonderful baked goods for giving as gifts. You can shop in Third-World shops or at the thrift stores in your town. By doing so, you give a thoughtful gift to your friend or relative and also support the poor.

2. Give the best. When you buy new toys or clothing for your children, buy the same toy or outfit for a needy child you don't know. Get lists of needed items from local orphanages, missionaries on furlough, family shelters, and day-care centers. Spend the same thought, effort, and money on your gifts to these organizations as you would on your own children. You'll feel better about what you give if you do.

3. Give of yourself. As much as money and material goods are needed, there is also a great need for people who are willing to get personally involved. Run errands; visit the poor with food baskets; help serve meals on Christmas Day. We sometimes get the mistaken idea that we can do our greatest service by simply giving money, but without loving hands to help, the money does not go as far as it might.

4. Work outside established channels. Do an act of kindness that is totally your own, unsponsored by your church or any other group. Look around you to see what can be done for a neighbor or shut-in. Get the name of some needy family from your pastor or your city's social service agency. Visit the family, find out what they need, and do your best to fill the need. Don't report what you did; don't include it on your charitable "resumé." Let your gift be just between you, the recipient, and God—no one else. It may even be possible to give anonymously. Savor the sweetness of silent giving, receiving no praise or recognition for what you have done.

If we want more joy in our giving, and if we want our gifts to be more worthwhile, we must examine every aspect of our lifestyle. We must concentrate not only on what we have given to others, but what we have kept for ourselves. The Bible story of the widow's mite—the old woman who was praised by Jesus for giving such a small offering—underscores the fact that it is not what we *give*, but what we *keep* that determines the value of our offering.

We will all keep for ourselves more than we need. But we can challenge ourselves, day by day and year after year, to close the gap between what we give and what we keep, and consequently between our expectations and our reality.

9

A Time for Churches

he idea of celebrating what we now refer to as Christmas stemmed from the church's decision to provide a Christian "cultural equivalent" for the converted pagans who were accustomed to a raucous winter festival. This practice began in the sixth century.

In later years (most specifically in the 1600s, at the time of Oliver Cromwell) there was a revolt by pious people who cried, "Enough!" and condemned the church-sponsored revelry as being incongruent with the teachings of Christ and an inappropriate commemoration of his birth.

That way of thinking prevailed in many circles until the 1800s, when there was a shift in opinion and a change of heart. Christmas was restored as a bona fide religious holiday, to the extent that today only a few Christians sects and some quasi-Christian cults have any serious objections to the church's present Christmas observances.

Certainly we all nurse some dissatisfactions with the holiday, and churches are often heard to proclaim (on lighted outdoor signs, Saturday-evening-newspaper advertisements, or somewhere in the weekly bulletin), "Let's put Christ back in Christmas!"

Let us put him back, indeed. But that plea begs the questions, "Where did he go? When did he go? Was he ever really there in the first place?"

We don't know the answers to these questions. But we do know instinctively that our Christmas celebrations are often lacking in spiritual vitality, and we look to the church—the church universal, as well as our local congregations—to do something about it. We don't know exactly what should be done, but we recognize the need.

In response to this spoken or unspoken mandate to "Put Christ back in Christmas," congregations plan and execute a plethora of activities, programs, and celebrations. They tend to take their cues from the most successful and interesting secular observances, decorating the sanctuary with beautiful fir trees and placing lovely pine boughs along the aisles. The minister may abandon his old black clerical robe in favor of a purple one for the Advent season or wear a bright red vest underneath his suitcoat. The everyday hymns are replaced by the singing of Christmas carols. Children rehearse for the Christmas Pageant, which nowadays is less likely to be the traditional Mary-Joseph-Babe-in-the-Manger program and more typically a peppy musical featuring little bugs, birds, and butterflies who present an obtuse allegory of the nativity or some such thing.

From November 30 on, there are Sunday School parties, pageant rehearsals, costumes to be fashioned, cookies to be baked, holiday clothing to be bought and sewn so our little cherubs will be as lovely as all the other little cherubs in the congregation, the special "something" we give to the pastor, caroling parties, cantata rehearsals and performances, and on and on and on with a million things to keep us busy during the Christmas holidays.

"Lord, help me survive the holidays!" prays the beleagured church member. With so much to be done and so few who will take responsibility, the church imposes on those who can be most easily persuaded to organize all the must-do activities. Our churches add to our holiday panic, failing in the areas where they should be strong and wasting themselves where they are unneeded.

Part of the problem—as has been pointed out before—is that there is little recognition of Advent. While it would be hard to attend, say, an Episcopalian or Catholic church during the month of December without realizing the arrival of the Advent season, in the majority of Protestant churches Advent simply doesn't exist. A few are now adding Advent wreath-lighting ceremonies to their morning worship—and that's a good sign, to be sure. But there is still a lack of Advent emphasis in the pulpit, and on the whole there is inadequate preparation for the arrival of the Christchild.

Then again, there are simply too many programs. Every church I have ever attended had, in my opinion, too much going on at Christmas. Perhaps this is due to the fact that we each get on our own bandwagon around the holidays and try to involve the congregation in our "thing."

The choir director wants to do a festive cantata; the Sunday School superintendent is planning a children's program; the Benevolence Committee is working on adopting a needy family; the Decorations Chairman has visions of a holly-decked sanctuary; the associate pastor has planned a special Wednesday-night Bible study on the Three Wisemen; the Social Committee (which has been functionally inactive for an entire year) has decided to serve cookies and coffee after the morning worship services between Thanksgiving and Christmas; the Ladies' Aid must finish up all those quilts and pinafores so they can be given to the orphanage; the Rebecca Circle is having a Christmas Flea Market to raise money; the Senior Highs are having a bake sale Sunday nights so they can go skiing; each Sunday School class is having a party.

Everybody wants to get into the act, and everybody is exhausted.

A third aspect of the problem is that there is little thought for the family at Christmas. At first glance it appears to be all family stuff. But take a closer look. The overabundance of activities wears away at the family. Why have family devotions? We have those at church. Why have family singing? We'll sing carols at church. Why invite anyone over to share the holidays? Everyone we care about is at church. Why show any act of kindness as a family? The Deacons' Fund is handling all that for us.

In addition to taking away our initiative, the fact that every night of the week is taken with some ecclesiastical preparation or activity means that family members will *not* be together. On Wednesdays Dad is at choir practice; on Saturday mornings the kids have to be taken to pageant rehearsal; the decorations will take all Friday evening and Saturday to position for Sunday morning. When is the whole family ever at home—together—during the Christmas season?

Guardians of Christmas

On a more positive note, then, what is the responsibility of the organized church regarding Christmas?

For the past two thousand years, the Christian church has kept the Scriptures safe, preserved the customs and traditions of believers, and proclaimed to each generation the Good News of Christ. The present-day church, then, must proclaim—year after year, without fail—the Good News of the birth of Christ. It must do so faithfully, stating the message correctly, simply, and clearly for everyone to hear.

In addition, it should provide a structure in which its members can find personal renewal and spiritual guidance throughout the holidays. For this reason, the lighting of the Advent wreath in worship services, the offering of seasonal devotional booklets, the providing of opportunities for service within the community—as long as their aim is to foster spiritual growth—become very important. Outreach programs, such as public performances of Christmas cantatas, benevolence programs, and public worship services, are also important. Sunday School programs whose ulterior motive is to lure nonattending parents of children into the sanctuary, Sunday School parties, and fund-raising bazaars are less important.

It's hard to say (and wrong to say) exactly how every church should involve itself in the celebration of Christmas. Based on varying traditions, congregational needs, and interpretations of the church's mission, there will be great latitude for many kinds of celebrative events in the life of the local church. But I firmly believe that each church should keep in mind that its traditional, historical function has been to act as guardian of the faith and proclaimer of the truth—and that doesn't change at Christmastime.

It is, then, the responsibility of the church—of individual believers and of organized bodies—to keep Christ in Christmas. It is not the duty of our government, our public schools, the greeting-card companies, or the department stores. They will do so only to the extent that we demand it or patronize them for it. It is up to *us*—the faithful—to keep the faith alive, to tell the true story of Christmas, to pass it on to our children.

If we are constantly aware of our mission, we will develop new celebrations in our churches. We will rise up in protest against meaningless time- and energy-consuming activities that contribute little to our mission. We won't make busywork for ourselves and others at Christmas, and we may resist the temptation to do so at other times of the year as well. Our children and young people will realize early that the church's observances reflect the spiritual dimension of Christmas. We will have more time for individual and corporate meditation, prayer, and reflection since we are spending less time running around doing everything and nothing.

What to Do, What to Do

It might be best at this point to just put the subject to rest and let each congregation decide what it will—and won't—do this Christmas on the basis of its perceived and stated mission. But there are too many good, positive activities that have been undertaken by church groups to let them go unannounced.

1. Have an *Unplug the Christmas Machine* workshop. As a companion of their book by the same name, Jo Robinson and Jean Staeheli have developed a four-hour seminar that can be given in churches (or to any other group). It may be offered on a Saturday morning or perhaps weekly for an hour per session during the four weeks of Advent. Its aim is to help members create family celebrations that are more in keeping with their resources, values, needs, and spiritual beliefs. Participants have an opportunity to isolate their holiday problems, define their goals, and create a simple plan to make their family Christmas a continuation of the vision they have in church.

Any interested and reasonably confident-in-front-of-people person can conduct the workshop, which is carefully outlined in the notebook that contains directions, timetables, planning guides, and handouts for participants. I highly recommend this workshop. Information about ordering materials is in the appendix.

2. Provide a devotional outline for members. In our church, members of the congregation are asked to write a short devotional message on an assigned passage of Scripture (assignments are given in July). The combined devotionals are then placed in a booklet and distributed to the congregation for use as an Advent devotional guide. Each devotional is signed (although they may be submitted anonymously), and readers get a unique spiritual glimpse into the life of the person who wrote each day's message. Some messages are hopeful, others share concerns and needs that are unmet. Some messages are profound doctrinally and theologically, while others are simple, heartfelt expressions. In addition to being a Christmas activity whose preparation is completely concluded by mid-November, thereby freeing people to concentrate on other matters, it is a binding influence that offers many members of the congregation an

opportunity to share something of their own faith and belief with others.

The pastor or a committee can prepare any number of devotional guides, perhaps using the traditional Scriptures of each day as recorded in *The Book of Common Prayer.*

3. Schedule activities sanely. Someone—the church secretary, the minister, someone!—should take on the responsibility for coordinating all church activities during the holiday season. More than at any other time of the year, some thought must be given to *when* activities are held, and *which* family members are most likely to be involved in them. Someone should have the power to force committee chairmen to reschedule or scrap events that threaten the sanity of the congregation.

In the workshop manual for *Unplug the Christmas Machine,* one woman is quoted as saying, "I asked if we could have our church activities over by December 16th this year so that I could salvage some time to be with my family. We're already going in twenty directions at once."

Consider guidelines such as "No church activities on Monday evenings or Saturdays" or "All Christmas activities completed by December 16 (or whenever)." The congregation and church staff must exercise discipline in this respect. As the child of a minister, I can attest to the fact that the pastor's family sees very little of the pastor during the holidays.

All of us who are church members can be instrumental in bringing our celebrations in line with the mission of the church. A word here or there, a suggestion, an alternative presented will go a long way toward making our congregational activities a positive, guiding force in our Christmas celebration.

10

A Time to Be Alone

sit there on the couch, and there are a million people in that house, and I grew up with half of them, and we all have a million children, and there are a million things going on, but no matter how many people there are and no matter how much confusion there is, I know that I am still absolutely, completely, unmistakenly alone."

"My terror begins in the middle of November, when the stores are starting to put up their decorations and sending out their Christmas catalogs, and people are planning their family celebrations for Thanksgiving. From that point on, I don't sleep well at night and I can't eat. I try not to think about what time of the year it is, because I know I am alone. I will be alone at Thanksgiving, and I will be alone at Christmas. I hate it. I'm alone."

"For fifty-one weeks of the year I dream about my kids being all grown-up and out of the house so that I can have some time to be with myself and start being my own person. My three kids drive me crazy most of the time. And then, a few days before Christmas, we have our presents, and our tree, and our Christmas dinner. Then I put them on the plane and they go to be with their father for the holidays. Ashley is only six-and-a-half, and she's really too young to make that trip. And after the plane has left, and I've waved it good-bye, and made my way through the terminal and back to my car, the pain in my gut makes me feel like I'm going to explode, and my jaw aches, and then I just cry and cry and cry. I'll have a whole week without my children. I know they're too young to make that trip."

"For the past three years I've spent Christmas alone. At first I didn't know if I'd have nerve enough to do it. I mean, our family has always been pretty close—at least we try to be—and if you *can* come home for Christmas, you're supposed to.

But I just couldn't hack it anymore; it was too much of a hassle. So for the last three years I just haven't gone. Mom and Dad accept it now, even though they don't understand exactly. I'm not saying that Christmas is terrific now that I'm doing this, but I think it's better. It's just something that I have to do for myself."

Christmas without family? you say. Christmas without friends? Christmas alone? No one should spend Christmas alone. It's too painful to even consider. No matter what it takes, no matter what kind of effort is involved, one simply must not spend Christmas alone. It's not right. It's totally against the spirit of Christmas.

If you don't believe it, just think back on all those *Saturday Evening Post* cover illustrations, with the big family gathered around the dining room table, eyes wide open at the sight of a twenty-six-pound Christmas turkey. Or look at the advertisements on television and in all the magazines. Why, those gloriously fulfilled people are celebrating Christmas with big families, with grandparents and little children. They are surrounded by their friends, happily munching on Chex Party Mix and drinking Canada Dry Ginger Ale. They are tucking their children into bed, they are pulling a pan of bar cookies out of the oven while great-grandma looks on, they are sitting together quietly on the couch enjoying a glass of wine. They are together; they are *not* alone.

So our ideal Christmas is garnished with people. No matter what else we wish for, it is that there be people surrounding us. It may be better friends or a magically transformed family, but there are people just the same.

The fact remains, however, that many of us are alone over the holidays. In a rare case, we find someone who is alone by choice, someone who has the opportunity to be with family and friends, but who makes a conscious decision to spend Christmas apart from these people—not for lack of money or opportunity, but simply by choice. This is certainly an exception. Even the most private, introverted, or shy person wants to step out and be with people at Christmastime—as a rule.

To be alone at Christmas is to experience perhaps the greatest conceivable disparity between expectation and reality—the expectation being that we will have a wonderful, warm, loving time with close family and friends, the reality being that we have neither family nor friends with whom to celebrate the holidays.

What's the solution? Some people hole up in their apartments, houses, or rented rooms. They do not attempt any kind of Christmas celebration because they believe that anything they try to do will only fail and further remind them that they don't have a "real" Christmas, and perhaps, because they are alone, they are not deserving of one anyway. They don't get a tree, don't send cards, don't make cookies, don't exchange presents. They simply ignore Christmas and hope that Christmas won't notice them.

Others make a gallant effort to do Christmas the way it's "supposed" to be, cooking a huge meal that they must eat all by themselves, trimming a tree that will shelter no presents, and decorating a home that no one will see. They create a celebration for other people—except the other people never come.

A few have come to grips with their aloneness. Whether they are alone in a crowd or truly isolated, they know that they are, for one reason or another, in a situation where they cannot and will not be sharing their celebration with others. Having defined their reality, they revise their expectations to bring them more in line with their reality, and similarly revise their reality so that it is to some extent more compatible with their expectations.

Those who are unmarried, separated, widowed, or divorced; whose parents are dead or living far away; who have no close friends that are "like family"; who have family problems that prevent festive gatherings; who for some reason feel out of sync with those around them—more than others, these people need to write their own script about how Christmas will be. They need to abandon useless and frustrating mental pictures of how Christmas looks and feels and smells and tastes. They need to open their eyes and see what their situation is and what their options can be. They need to quit setting before themselves an unobtainable goal, an unreached standard.

When faced with Christmas alone we must, for our own sakes, set aside false visions of the past and look for fulfillment in the very real present. We must work toward a healthy celebration. We must muster strength to carry out some modest changes.

All Alone in A Crowd

There is in most of us a yearning to be alone, even when we are with others. We are with people—at work, at home, at church, in our neighborhood—so much during the holidays that we begin to fantasize about having a moment or two only for ourselves. We want time to relax, time to read, time to watch television, time to putter around the house—alone!

But we don't get that time. There is always something drawing us away from ourselves: people need us; people invite us over for dinner; people want us to attend the school Christmas play; people ask for help wrapping presents; people need and want, so we provide.

If we want to fulfill our need to be alone, we must exercise aloneness as a discipline. One may need to force oneself to say "no" to a party, "no" to a child's demands, "no" to a lunch invitation.

You say, "I don't want to be lonely." The truth is that you will indeed feel lonely when alone unless you have an "alone self" that can survive not only the hubbub but the quietness as well.

When I am uncomfortable with who I really am, then I don't want to be alone with myself. I would rather surround myself with a lot of activity in order to avoid having to face myself. Some people do this their entire lives. Others find that the spiritual challenge of celebrating Christ's birthday is better dealt with by drowning him out with a myriad of people and activities than by confronting the nativity event.

Yet, we must find our "alone self" in the Christmas holidays. If we can, we will emerge in the month of January less disappointed, less depressed, less vague.

You have a planning calendar that we worked on in Chapter 4. (You have a planning calendar!) Is there time on the calendar for yourself, alone? Glance over it once again to assure yourself that each day isn't so crammed with activities that there isn't sufficient time to collect yourself by yourself. Some people require only ten to fifteen minutes to refresh themselves; others need up to several hours a day in self-imposed solitary confinement before they can face the world. It depends on how you're put together. But you need some time to divorce yourself from all the hubbub around you and to get in touch with your "alone self." The amount of time you require will be your personal, individual balance between time alone and time with others.

What should you do when you are alone? Here are some ideas:

—Take a nap.
—Read a book or magazine.
—Read Christmas cards.
—Listen to a record.
—Do a puzzle—crossword, jigsaw, hidden word . . .
—Read your Bible.
—Pray.
—Meditate.
—Write in your diary or journal.
—Have a cup of coffee and a cookie.
—Go for a walk.
—Exercise—calisthenics, weights, jogging . . .
—Look out the window and daydream.
—Take a pleasure drive.
—Visit the library.
—Go to a movie.
—Shovel snow or sweep the sidewalk.

It may take a great deal of discipline and determination to sit down and thumb through a magazine when you should be Doing Something. But you can do something later. Now it is important for you to nourish your "alone self," because if it doesn't survive all the activity, the rest of you will perish as well.

Alone & Feeling Lonely

It's all very well to talk about how to find some time for oneself amidst all the confusion and activity of the holidays, but what about those of us who are truly alone? We don't need to make time for our "alone self" because we are always alone.

We live in isolation. We would gladly trade our unhappy aloneness and loneliness for the challenge of finding a few minutes for ourselves in the middle of the demands of other people. We would much rather have to turn down an invitation for one party because we're already going out that evening than sit at home alone night after night with nothing to do. We crave intimacy. We would eagerly welcome the opportunity to be with our extended family—no matter how boisterous, how thoughtless, how exhausting—rather than spend another holiday in solitude.

The irony of all this is that those who are alone are often timid about asking around, investigating, and making plans with others who are also alone. It is as though it's bad enough to be alone at Christmas, but even worse to let the fact be known.

Lack of candor about one's wish to be with others nearly always results in maintenance of the status quo—that is, loneliness. For while many people would be glad to include a single friend or two in their family celebration, and many single people would like to band together with other singles to create a family situation, the fact that alone people are embarrassed about their status prevents their need being expressed and consequently met.

This reticence to make one's position known is completely understandable. When you are alone at Christmas, you are not merely having to come to grips with a few days when you'd rather be with people. You are dealing afresh with the fact that you are widowed, orphaned, unwanted, deserted, abandoned, isolated. Is all that true? Well, whether or not it's verifiable, that's how you feel.

A widow who has dealt with the biggest part of her grief over losing her husband, who has made enormous strides toward self-confidence and self-sufficiency, who has worked toward combating the loneliness she feels by the loss of her lifelong mate, may find herself taking a giant step backward in her "development" during the Christmas holidays. Everything she has told herself and believed about herself comes into question. She thought she was independent and capable, but how will she ever select and erect the tree? She thought she was self-confident, but does she have enough nerve to entertain the old crowd without him? She thought she was happy, but there will be tears when it's all over and she faces the fact that there was no present from him.

I have three convictions about The Art of Spending Christmas Alone.

1. You needn't deal with all your issues at this time. This holds true for anyone who is working through hurt, disappointment, crisis, and tough problems. Although Christmas can be a growing time, it should have that function only insofar as you are able to handle such growth emotionally, psychologically, spiritually, and physically.

The widow, for example, will eventually have to learn to do a great number of tasks by herself that she used to do with her husband. But in the interest of making it through the holidays in one piece, she can smooth the way for herself in a number of simple ways. She can ask a nursery (or a neighbor) to deliver a nice tree and set it up for her, instead of picking it out and setting it up herself. She doesn't have to entertain her friends if it will be painful to do so—at least not this year. If he usually bought her a negligee or perfume for Christmas, she can go out and buy them for herself this year, and confront later the gaping hole his death has left in her life.

It's okay—it's helpful—to overlook some of your major disappointments and problems at Christmastime and concentrate instead on what you have going for you. You don't have to tackle major issues. You don't have to come to grips with all your problems. You don't have to work through all your frustrations. You don't have to be strong. You can look for some easy answers, some psychological band-aids, if it will help you cope. Later—as the days, weeks, and months go by—under less stressful circumstances, you can be brutally honest with yourself, you can exercise the discipline you need, you can heal the old wounds. It is often difficult for even the most together, most secure, most mentally healthy person to make it through the Christmas holiday with his good humor intact. Don't place a burden on yourself that is too great to bear.

2. Finding others with whom you can celebrate is worth the risk.

Vast numbers of people don't believe this. Because of their hurt, timidity, or fear of rejection, they are unwilling to make phone calls, visit neighbors, question co-workers, or invite themselves to participate in the celebrations of others. They are afraid of being turned down: "Oh, no, I can't come over to your place for Christmas Day. Well, my goodness, I'm going to my sister's house on the 23rd and staying over through New Year's, as I do *every* year!" or patronized: "Well, I have plans, but if you'd like to join us I could maybe ask Wilfred, and if it's okay with him . . ."

There is also the fear that we will find someone who accepts the invitation. Then what? How will you be able to reconcile your expectations with that of another person, perhaps someone who is almost a stranger to you? What if it doesn't work out? What if you have a dreadful, horrible time? What if they're accepting only to be polite? "Oh, it would never work. I'll just stay home, like always . . ."

Over the years there have been times when Steve or I were alone for a holiday: Easter, Thanksgiving, Christmas. Finding others who would celebrate the holidays with us wasn't easy. When we were in seminary, we celebrated one Easter with about six other students—foreign students who didn't understand why they were being asked to decorate eggs, or why the butter was in the shape of a lamb. They couldn't converse well in English, and I can't say it was a rip-roaring good time. I suppose the best that can be said about it is that it was memorable.

Other times I've had visions of setting a beautiful table for fifteen or twenty people, all of whom would be simply thrilled to spend the holidays with us. Instead, admitting in my first phone call that I was alone and was trying to get something going for Thanksgiving Day, I was invited to take part in another person's celebration, forcing me to abandon my hopes of entertaining and instead become only a participant (as opposed to choreographer) in a Thanksgiving meal where they put the milk carton right on the table and served everything out of Tupperware—hardly what I had my heart set on.

More than once a dozen phone calls yielded a dozen rejections, and I had to celebrate alone after all. So there is a risk. Still, I do believe that the hope of fellowship is definitely worth the risk and that the worst that can happen is that you won't be able to find anyone to celebrate with. But then at least you're no worse off than when you started.

On the other hand, what might happen could be wonderful. I believe that some of the nicest holidays I've had were times when I either invited or accepted an invitation from someone I didn't know very well or whose celebration was very different from my own.

One single woman related that her greatest dread was waking up Christmas morning to her empty apartment, having no one to eat breakfast or open presents with. Finally she hit on the idea of having a few friends over for Christmas Eve, and then inviting one or two to spend the night. When she woke up there was at least one other person there to help scramble the eggs and propose a toast of eggnog, making all the difference in the world in how she felt on Christmas Day.

A mother whose children spend the holidays with her ex-husband celebrates Christmas with one of her brothers or a cousin. She is known to be available for a week at Christmastime to whatever family would like an extra pair of hands to wash dishes, wrap packages, run errands, and generally help out. By being so useful, she is in great demand with relatives who issue enthusiastic invitations, asking her to spend Christmas with them. The activity helps her combat her loneliness.

One elderly woman has over the years contacted young couples and single people in her church who cannot be with their families at Christmas. Unable to do all the preparations necessary for feeding a crowd, she invites them over for a Christmas Day potluck dinner and revels in having her empty house filled to the rafters with the sound of children's laughter and young people's discussions from 10:00 in the morning until 10:00 at night. Many of her guests come year after year; others attend only when they don't have anything else to do. She doesn't mind being second choice. The word is out about her gala event, and anyone who sees that they are going to be alone knows they can just call her up and invite themselves over on Christmas Day.

3. Helping others takes the sting out of being alone. Women facing an empty nest know that volunteer work is an excellent way of filling their lives with useful and appreciated work. Those who are physically handicapped often find fulfillment and satisfaction in helping those who have a similar disability. People who have survived heart attacks or cancer may be the only ones who can help those who are still struggling with their disease.

There are many, many people in any community who need special care, attention, and service over the holidays. Who will care for the abused women and children at the Family Shelter? Who will man the crisis lines? Who will serve meals to transients and the homeless at the Salvation Army? Who will visit the elderly in nursing homes who have outlived all their friends and relatives?

A great way to deal with your own problems is to help someone else with theirs. Such activity is not just therapy for you; it is an important service to those in need.

There are some jobs that must be done even though it's Christmas: twenty-four-hour restaurants need waitresses and cooks; hospitals and nursing homes need doctors, nurses, and aides; drugstores need pharmacists; cities need firefighters and police officers. Many industries proceed business-as-usual on Christmas Day. The person who will be alone on the holidays has an excellent opportunity to show concern and friendship for co-workers with families by volunteering to work their holiday shift. The favor can be repaid when you have a better opportunity to enjoy the time off.

"Go Away. I Want to Be Alone."

Can you picture this?

—Christmas in a rustic seaside cabin, sketching the landscape and seascape, eating shrimp and lobster, catching up on sleep.

—Christmas holed up in your apartment with a pile of magazines you haven't gotten around to reading, a pantry full of your favorite foods, and a freezer stuffed with Stouffer's frozen entrées and Sara Lee cheesecake and croissants.

—Christmas skiing in Switzerland.

—A twenty-four-hour prayer and meditation vigil that begins 6:00 Christmas Eve and ends at the same time Christmas Day.

—Christmas in New York City, attending plays, eating in fine restaurants, visiting museums.

Each possibility probably sounds like a pretty good option for someone who is *forced* to spend Christmas by themselves. But lately more and more people who have ample opportunity to spend the holidays with family and friends are *choosing* to spend that time alone instead.

It's a difficult decision to make. No matter how intrigued you might be with the idea of buying one round-trip ticket to the Alps and celebrating Christmas on the slopes, the prospect of informing your parents, your friends, and your in-laws that you're taking off on your own for Christmas is frightening. Besides, what if you hate it? What if you have a miserable time skiing? What if there aren't any other people there for you to celebrate with? It could be a total fiasco.

But if you have spent the weeks leading up to Christmas managing an extra-heavy holiday workload, if you feel emotionally alienated from your family and friends, if you crave solitude and are unable to find it in your traditional observances, if you sense that you are in a growing place and that it is important for you to have a private Christmas observance, then you have already seriously considered the advantages of going it alone at Christmas.

The first thing to do is to identify your reasons for wanting to spend Christmas alone. Write them out if that helps. After you have articulated your reasons, try to assess their validity. Ask yourself, "Am I being fair to myself and my friends/family when I make that statement? Am I denying some other problem? Is this the best way? Am I really likely to get what I need out of spending Christmas alone?"

Next, make a plan. You should plan what you are going to do at Christmas—whether you are at home or away—and plan how you are going to notify your family and friends of your decision. The last part could be the most difficult of all. Will your children understand why you won't be at their house this year—even though you only live thirteen blocks away and have no other plans than staying at home all day, listening to old records? Since you have defined your reasons and satisfied yourself that they are valid, you will have some idea about what you're going to tell them. It's probably best not to turn it into a knockdown, drag-out, hair-pulling fight about solitude and independence. Be as evenhanded about it as you can; there is already enough emotion inherent in the decision itself.

Lastly, give yourself an "out." Let Daddy know that if it doesn't work out, you'll come over later in the day; find out about any get-togethers your friends are having and that you might attend at the last minute; don't make any plane or hotel reservations that you can't cancel if you have to. This is no time to be dropped by helicopter into the Canadian wilderness, with instructions to be picked up again on December 28. Keep your options open; you might have to exercise them.

There's no way of knowing whether or not you'll enjoy spending Christmas alone until you do it. It's obvious that the opportunities for personal prayer, meditation, and reflection are greater alone, and that exercising these disciplines could be the key to transforming Christmas from a jumble of meaningless and tiring activities into a rich spiritual experience.

To be alone at Christmas, either by choice or default, either in a crowd or true isolation, has potential for fulfillment as well as emptiness. It contains elements of happiness as well as sadness.

We all have a need to develop our "alone self" and our "social self." Those whose holiday season is a blur of people washing in and out in a reckless, never-ending stream need to find time to be alone, just as those who have no one need to find someone. Christmas alone has risks and dangers. It also has tremendous opportunity. Each individual must find her own balance, her own niche, working as always at the task of reconciling expectations and reality.

11

The Singular Christmas

t's that out-of-whack Christmas. The one that doesn't happen the way it's supposed to happen. The one that isn't right. It's the Christmas when you're in bed with pneumonia; when your kids don't come home for the holidays for the first time; when your husband is out of work; when you're broke. Here's what I mean:

"Ironically, Suzanne chose Christmas Day to announce she was leaving me. I had no idea that it was coming, so it truly hit hard. Why me, why is this happening, why on Christmas Day, why, why, why?"

"One week before Christmas, Katie was diagnosed as having retinal blastoma—a rare form of cancer. Our six-month-old daughter was operated on, had one of her eyes removed, and faced a regimen of laser therapy for the remaining tumors."

"Our Christmas experience in Africa was somewhat astonishing. We went 'up-country' with friends to their family home in a rural area. The two of us shared a single (not twin, but single) bed in a house with mud walls and cow-dung floor, waking on Christmas Day to the sound of drums, having no presents, no decorations, nothing but church and family togetherness."

"How does one endure that first Christmas after the death of a loved one—my husband? Our family rarely said what we were thinking or feeling. I guess we just hoped someone would know what we wanted or needed. That cold Christmas morning I kept hoping they would realize what I was feeling and just leave me be."

"One Christmas Eve we were invited out of town—to Seattle. The time there was fun with friends, but coming home on Christmas Day to an unfestive house was depressing. Equally depressing was eating week-old leftovers for our meal. Yuck."

"It was the only time we hadn't been able to go to our parents' house for Christmas. I was expecting a baby in January, and we had planned on making the trip, even though it was getting late in my pregnancy. On December 22 I went to the doctor for my checkup. I was developing complications. He told me to go home and go to bed; I was to stay in bed, resting on my left side. I was to keep calm—no excitement. I couldn't even get up to eat. He consented to letting me get up to go to the bathroom, but that was all. Christmas went down the drain."

"I had it in mind that we had to get moved into our new house before Christmas. For some reason it was very important to me. We worked toward that goal, and we actually did get moved in, after a fashion. At least we were sleeping there. But we expended all our energy on the move and didn't have anything left for the celebration. Everything was in boxes and I hadn't been able to do any baking, there were no decorations, the place was a mess."

You've probably had one or two "odd" Christmases in your life so far, and you will certainly have a few more in the future. Things happen that you can't help; certain events are beyond your control. You find yourself—and your Christmas—at the mercy of an illness, a forced separation from family or friends, the death of a loved one, or some other tragedy.

If reality won't cooperate, expectations can be modified. Your outlook can be changed. It's best to approach the problem systematically.

Put It in Perspective

It is tempting to overstate the case when holiday happiness is threatened by an unexpected turn of events. Before dealing effectively with the situation at hand, problems must be put in perspective. That involves coming to the place where you can say:

1. **"I will survive."** Say this with sincerity. If you simply cannot, seek help immediately—from a counselor, your minister, a competent friend. In the case of severe trauma or crisis, you may very well feel that you will not make it through, that you will perish under the strain. If this is your sincere belief, get the help you need.

But if you're in the hospital with a leg in traction, if you're spending your first Christmas in the Army, if you have to work a double shift on Christmas Eve, it shouldn't be too hard to believe that you'll survive. An honest moment or two with yourself will convince you of the fact that the situation is not beyond your coping capabilities.

2. **"This one Christmas is different."** This is one Christmas out of your life. The *event* that is causing the problem may be one that will change your entire life, as in the case of divorce or death of a loved one or a serious injury. But right now we're only thinking about Christmas. Today's challenge is how to survive Christmas in light of these special circumstances. You don't have to deal with all your painful issues at this time. For now, it's enough to accept the fact that—like it or not—this Christmas is different.

3. **"This, too, shall pass."** It can't last forever. Christmas will come and go; the problem you face will—to some extent—come and go. It will pass.

Look for Possibilities

Even the most hopeless situations contain possibilities. Your first thoughts may be that there are no options, or none that you are interested in. If you let your thinking stop there, you're doomed. Discipline yourself to look beyond the obvious and discover the hidden.

1. **View the situation.** What's going on? Can you define the situation? Try to be objective. You might make statements like:

"I lost my job; consequently I don't have money for celebrating."

"My wife seems determined to move out of the house."

"My child is extremely ill."

2. Analyze the situation, with a view to uncovering possibilities. Then you can say:

"Since I don't have any discretionary funds—which would definitely be needed to celebrate as I have done in the past—I'm going to have to figure out some other way to have a meaningful Christmas."

"If Suzanne is insistent upon leaving, I'm going to have to figure out how to do a number of things: talk to our son about what's happened, break the news to our family, take care of the day-to-day things that she usually does."

"Donny can't leave the hospital, so we won't be able to have the same kind of Christmas morning we usually have. This will be difficult for all of us. We'll have to find a way to have what fun we can."

3. Brainstorm. List ideas—by yourself, writing them down on paper, working with a friend, or as a family—that come to mind. At this point, they don't all have to be good or even possible. Just relax and let ideas come into your head.

"There are lots of festive things that don't cost any money. Everything going on at church is free—the cantata, the Sunday School party, the special Advent services. I have some scrap lumber in the basement; I might be able to make some presents out of that. The union has an emergency fund; perhaps there's some money to be had there. Janelle might have a dress I could borrow and wear to Stanley and Joan's party."

"I'm going to call up Darryl and see if he'll have lunch with me. I can tell him all about Suzanne leaving. I know he'll be a good shoulder to cry on. Tory has always wanted to stay overnight with my mom; I'll call her, explain the situation, and see if he can spend the weekend with her while I sort things out. I'll ask Sis to come over Thursday and help me with the housekeeping. I've got to find some time to be by myself and decide what to do."

"I can bring Donny's woodburning set to the hospital, and he could make some Christmas decorations; I'll ask the nurses if we can all come in and surprise him on Christmas morning with his packages. Maybe some of the other kids in the hospital would like to get involved. We could have a party. I wonder if he can have a tree in his room? I'll bring over the Penney's catalog and let him pick out gifts for his sisters. Then he can wrap them himself. Maybe the doctor will say he won't have to have his therapy on Christmas Day—that way he won't feel so tired."

Engage the Possibilities

The Singular Christmas—like every other Christmas—ultimately presents many more possibilities than can reasonably be implemented. The list will have to be trimmed down to size. At first glance you may have thought that your exceptional situation robbed you of options; further examination almost always reveals that the opportunities are nearly endless. It's still a matter of determining what—out of many things—you'll do.

Decide what is feasible. Take into consideration your mental, emotional, and physical energy, your material resources, the availability of help from family and friends. For example, the mother with a hospitalized child can probably think of a thousand ways to bring Christmas to the hospital, but only a few are practical. So she decides that she could fix her child up with some handcraft projects that keep him occupied during the days before Christmas, when she is very busy and doesn't have as much time to be with him and entertain him. Her family isn't too keen on the idea of getting up early and trekking over to the hospital on Christmas Day, and neither is the hospital administration. Instead, they decide to go to the hospital after they've had a chance to open their gifts. Then they'll exchange with Donny. They'll bring cookies and small gifts for the other boys in his room.

Expect Serendipity

When fortunate discoveries are made by accident, that's serendipity. How can one expect an accident? You can't, really. But in nearly every instance, the person who has approached the exceptional Christmas situation with a positive attitude has been pleased to discover that there was something pleasant, something warm, something worthwhile hidden beneath the disappointing, disconcerting, or even tragic circumstances that threw his Christmas out-of-whack.

Positive outcomes are most likely to occur if you can relax and respond.

Relax

Having come to an awareness that this too shall pass, you can let go of the nervousness and fear that is blocking your ability to find the good in the situation. Relax. Meditate and pray. Stare out of the window, take a walk, have a cup of tea, relax. Clear your thoughts of problems and issues too big to be dealt with right now. Knowing you'll survive, relax.

Respond

See what is going on around you that is positive, and take part in it. Enter into what is happening.

The couple who spent Christmas in rural Africa shared: "We found we did miss the trappings of Christmas in America—even missed the shopping malls and the parking lots and the Perry Como crooning. It was hard to feel Christmas without those familiar things. Still and all, those African Christmases stand out in memory very strongly; though they lacked the feel of Christmas, they were times when we learned a lot and made some deep friendships. Maybe the lesson is not to work too hard at re-creating the past, but to be aware of what is happening now."

The sad thing is that a longing for the past is often the biggest obstacle to appreciating the present.

The young father whose wife asked for a divorce on Christmas Day said: "I eventually could see that Christmas is Jesus' birthday, and no amount of material joy or human pain should deviate from that. Suddenly I wasn't taking it for granted. So many people, with more normal situations, do take it for granted. In that respect, it has been good for me."

Does it sound trite to say that there is some good to be found in any situation? Perhaps it does. But the witness of those who have gone through some extremely difficult times indicates that it's true nonetheless.

Sometimes the serendipity, the good, is immediately apparent. A woman who spent Christmas at the hospital bedside of her terminally ill husband was visited with an unspeakable sense of peace and fulfillment as she kept vigil with her partner of fifty years. As she sat there, she knew it was the best Christmas they had ever celebrated in their many years together.

Sometimes it takes years to see what the good was. To the extent that you can relax and respond, you can expect serendipity— or at least not be shocked if it occurs.

It was my niece Katie who had retinal blastoma at the age of six months, who underwent surgery only days before Christmas, and who lost an eye to that rare form of cancer. She was released from the hospital for Christmas, but the close brush with death and the uncertainty we all felt for her future health cast a shadow over our holiday celebration that year.

But our anxiety changed to comfort on Christmas Eve when we received a letter and photograph from another couple whose infant child had suffered the same ordeal. The photo was of a beautiful little two-year-old girl. The letter was filled with hope and encouragement: that there is effective treatment for the disease, that healing is possible, that the bandages come off and normal childhood begins.

Those of us who have experienced and survived the Singular Christmas—the out-of-whack Christmas—are uniquely qualified to help others through their hard places. We can say to others who are struggling with what, for them, is tragedy, "You will survive. This one Christmas is different. But it too shall pass. Look for possibilities, and engage those possibilities. And don't be surprised if something wonderful happens . . ."

12

Epiphany

hey went on their way, and the star they had seen in the east went ahead of them until it stopped over the place where the child was. When they saw the star, they were overjoyed. On coming to the house, they saw the child with his mother Mary, and they bowed down and worshiped him. Then they opened their treasures and presented him with gifts of gold and of incense and of myrrh" (Matthew 2:9-11).

The visit of the Magi, or Wise Men, probably took place two years after the birth of Christ. The church has traditionally celebrated the event twelve days after Christmas and called that day Epiphany.

Epiphany means "to appear or be manifest." The significance of Epiphany for Christians is that the visit of the Magi represents the fact that Christ came not only for the Jews, but appeared to the Gentiles—and the rest of the world—as well. The Wise Men symbolize the manifestation of Jesus as the Christ to all people; this marks a turning-point in history. This event completes the Christian holiday of Christmas. The Messiah was awaited, and we relive the waiting during Advent. The Messiah came, and on Christmas Eve and Day we celebrate the arrival. The Messiah brought salvation for all mankind, and on Epiphany we are reminded that his birth launches a new era for each of us.

Epiphany, then, is observed on January 6, also known as Twelfth Day or Twelfth Night. The old song about the twelve days of Christmas speaks to the custom of beginning—not ending—the Christmas celebration on December 25, and continuing it for twelve more days until January 6.

"Ugh," you say. "I couldn't bear the thought of dragging Christmas on through January. It's like having mashed potatoes and gravy for breakfast! By the time it's December 26, I'm ready to get that dry old tree out of the house, put the presents away, throw out the stale cookies, and get back to business as usual. I've had enough fudge and eggnog to make me sick, enough parties to exhaust me, and enough presents to make me wish I'd never seen a Christmas bow! Save me from the Twelve Days of Christmas!"

Christmas Before

Before Cabbage Patch Dolls, Chevis Regal, Trivial Pursuit, and He-Man Action Figures were the pivot-point of Christmas, holiday celebrations started a day or two before Christmas Day with some preparatory baking and small gift wrapping, and celebrants were glad to extend the festivities and merrymaking a full twelve days into the new year. And why not? In a primarily rural, agrarian society there was little work to do during the cold, dark days of the winter solstice. The old custom of the Yule Log was part of that tradition: on Christmas Eve, the servants (or slaves) of the household would go out and gather the biggest, greenest, wettest log they could find—the Yule Log. As long as it burned and smoldered in the fireplace of the master's house, they were excused from their normal duties or had to be paid extra for any essential work they did do. Of course, that practice was built around the idea that the celebration of Christmas should go on and on and on. And for the servants at least, there was an obvious incentive to make it last as long as humanly possible.

But now that our celebration involves so much buying, wrapping, early mailing, entertaining, decorating, cooking, and general preparing, we must anticipate Christmas well in advance of the day. Needlepoint kits for counted cross-stitch Christmas tree ornaments are displayed in July and August; Christmas candy sits alongside Halloween goodies in October; downtown street decorations are in place by the middle of November; retail merchants say the biggest day of the year for sales is the day after Thanksgiving. Most of us agree that all of this shamelessly rushes the season. Nevertheless, we go along with it to a certain extent, and by the time December 26 rolls around, we've pretty much had our fill of Christmas.

For the most part, just about everything is set up for a Christmas season that sees Christmas Day as the finale of the production, not the overture. And although it simply wouldn't be Christmas for most of us without clicking our tongues, shaking our heads, and remarking ruefully about the way the whole world shamelessly rushes the season, we buy into that timetable more than we care to admit. And because we do, we're plenty glad to strip the mantel of its garland, toss the cards in the trash, and return all the duplicate gifts well before New Year's Day. We've had enough.

Christmas After: The Hidden Solution

"I feel letdown after Christmas is over. I've done so much work—and then what? Nothing. No more parties, no more gifts, no more decorations, no more excitement. I suppose I like Christmas so much that I can't stand to see it end. I'm always left with a feeling that something that was supposed to happen didn't."

"Figuring out what to do with the kids after Christmas is a big problem in our house. It's really true what they say about how all the toys get broken by the day after Christmas. They do. Or important parts get thrown away with the wrapping paper, or the batteries wear down, or the kids get frustrated with them because the toys are too advanced or whatever. I wish they could go back to school right away. But there's a week of torture between Christmas and New Year's when all the excitement is over, and they don't know what to do with themselves."

"It seems ridiculous to me that business is conducted in this country during the week between Christmas and New Year's. That's a dead week if ever there was one. Half the work force has decided to take a week of vacation then, and the other half just drags into work. There's high absenteeism—people taking sick days before the year is over so they don't lose what they've accumulated, not to mention people who really *are* sick from all the celebrating. Many of the mothers can't come in to work because their children are out of school and someone has to watch out for them. I have to go into the office because I'm in management, and someone *has* to be in charge. But little work gets done. It's the same story at all the other companies; so you can't get anyone on the phone. The whole thing seems ludicrous to me."

"I'm one of those people who gets sick every year after Christmas. All the excitement, no sleep, rich foods, lack of exercise, and the change in my everyday routine take their toll on me until I get sick. Usually it's a cold. Depending on how strenuous the holidays have been, it could be a flu-like thing, or bronchitis. Once I got pneumonia. I can count on spending a few days in bed after Christmas. If I'm lucky, I'll get better by New Year's Eve."

The paradox of Epiphany is that while we might have an aversion to continuing the celebration of Christmas on into January because we've had enough, it could well be that just a little more is the secret to ending the holidays sanely, so that when it's all over, we can look back and say what we all want to say: "This really was a great Christmas."

Many of the frustrations and problems we face with Christmas have to do with the fact that a tremendous amount of time, energy, planning, and money are invested in a twenty-four-hour extravaganza that is, as we have noted throughout this book, unable to live up to our expectations. But what if all our expectations didn't have to be met during the period from 5:00 P.M. December 24 to 5:00 P.M. December 25? What if we had days and days in which to make our dreams come true?

That would be to redefine *Christmas* to mean, "December 25 and the twelve days following it." During that time period, we could spread out our feasting, our game-playing, our visiting, our worship, our fun.

But how can we do that? We are too exhausted to let it go on that long. We've had enough.

The obvious answer is that we could conscientiously adjust our pre-Christmas pace. We must not, for example, do all our entertaining, make all our cookies, visit all our friends, or have all our family times together before Christmas Day. We must save some of those experiences until *after* December 25. "It won't work," you say.

Ah, but it will . . .

Good to the Last Drop

If you want Christmas to last, if you want to celebrate on through Epiphany (or thereabouts), if you want to complete the spiritual emphasis begun in Advent, you will probably need to make changes. Most of these will involve rescheduling some ordinarily pre-Christmas activities for after Christmas Day. It might take some discipline. When you see the chocolate-chip, candied fruit, and mixed nut displays at the supermarket, you will have to remind yourself that there's plenty of time for that sort of thing—*later*. When the Christmas tree lots begin to appear in abandoned filling stations, you must tell yourself that you'll get your tree a little *later*. When you begin to wonder if you shouldn't organize some little get-togethers with your friends, you must make a mental note to do so—*later* on.

What a coup for procrastinators, for sidetracked organizers, and exhausted celebrators! If you find the weeks before Christmas rushed and frantic, or if you tend to want to put off essential types of activities until some other time, Epiphany is for you! You needn't do less or more; just spread it out and do it at a more leisurely pace. Once you've decided what to do during the Christmas season, you will have greater options as to when it will be done.

If any extended celebration appeals to you, read on. The following are some practical suggestions to get you started. Don't attempt an all-in-one-year, complete overhaul. One or two things at a time, remember.

1. Save the baking or making of three of your favorite holiday foods for after Christmas.

2. Cut your own Christmas tree so it will be fresh enough to last until Epiphany.

3. Trim your Christmas tree the old-fashioned way: do it on Christmas Eve. The decorating of your tree and your home can be the focus of your Christmas Eve activities.

4. After Christmas, decorate an outdoor tree with popcorn or bread cubes on string or homemade suet balls as a gift to the birds and wildlife. Maintain the tree throughout the winter.

5. Open Christmas presents at the rate of one per day throughout the twelve days of Christmas. This is a great way to help children keep from getting so frantic and burned-out on Christmas Day.

6. Save all your entertaining for after Christmas. Enjoy attending the church and social functions to which you are invited before Christmas, and do your own parties after. Friends will appreciate

your invitations when they don't compete with other preholiday commitments.

7. Make table games or sporting equipment of some kind a part of your Christmas giving. These are presents that can be enjoyed by the recipients well into the new year.

8. Send out your Christmas cards after the holidays.

9. Write letters—either on your own or with your family—during the twelve days of Christmas. Catch up on your correspondence; thank those who sent you gifts; renew an old friendship.

10. Plan outings. Here are some suggestions: sledding, tobogganing, or cross-country skiing; a visit to an art gallery; a day at the library. St. Stephen's Day is December 26 and has been the traditional day to do something that involves animals. You might plan a trip to the zoo, a hunting expedition, horseback riding, or a visit to a natural science museum on St. Stephen's Day.

11. Plan a big project that will last through Epiphany. You could work on a family cookbook, compiling old favorites that have been handed down through the generations as well as new recipes. Sort through the year's snapshots, putting them in photo albums with captions and dates. Build a birdhouse or feeder. Give serious attention to an ambitious craft project: crochet an afghan, knit a sweater, tie that quilt top that's been sitting around for six years, embroider a set of pillowcases, sew doll clothes, make stuffed animals. Pace yourself so the project will be completed on January 6. Plan some ceremony to mark its completion.

12. Children can collect the discarded trees of neighbors and build a fort out of them that will keep them occupied until they go back to school.

13. Make an event of untrimming your Christmas tree and undecorating your house or apartment. Ask friends to help. Play the

Christmas records for the final time. Finish up the cookies and candy. Eat the last of the ham or turkey. Share your best holiday experiences with each other.

14. It has been traditional to remove all holiday greenery from the home and burn it on January 5. Depending on where you live, and the codes regulating open fires, you might make a custom of having a bonfire fueled by Christmas garland and trees—your own and your neighbors'.

And a Happy New Year

Since ancient times, New Year's Eve has been an occasion to drive out the old evil, and New Year's Day has been the time to usher in the good. Toward this end, people throughout history and in nearly every modern culture have devised scores of customs and rituals designed to make sure that every devil and evil spirit is gone with the old year, and that the new starts out on the right foot.

Our noisemaking and fireworks all derive from ancient customs of exorcism of this type. Whether it's pealing church bells or squealing party horns, we want to find a way to loudly ring out the old and welcome in the new.

In that sense, New Year's is a rite of passage. As any year draws to a close, we are apt to characterize it as the one that was "sad for me," or "an important year," or "the year when all the kids were finally out of the house," or "the year we had such a nice summer vacation." Consequently, we wish to cap off the events of the past year in some way, making it clear to ourselves that what has been done is now behind us.

Having done so, we look to the future. When New Year's Day arrives, we are ready to make a few resolutions: we'll lose ten pounds, or take a night class at the university this year, or mend fences with a neighbor, or get the basement paneled. Life starts over, in a sense, and we want to commemorate the event that annually lets us start afresh.

If you would like to mark that ending and beginning more specifically and meaningfully, try one or two of the following:

1. This year, make a New Year's resolution that you will *want* to keep. Several years ago I vowed to sample each and every kind of pie offered at a nearby restaurant that featured about twenty varieties. How about a resolution to see ten movies in the coming year, to get a season ticket for the symphony, to spend less time and effort on housework?

2. Have a party or reception at your house from 8:00 to 10:00 on New Year's Eve, and when all your guests have gone to other celebrations, enjoy a quiet time by yourself or with a friend or spouse while you welcome the new year.

3. Organize your church's New Year's celebration. Ask several people to host parties in their homes that will disband at 11:00 so everyone can meet together at the church for a Watch Night Service and Communion.

4. Spend New Year's Eve Day getting rid of the old. For example: Clean out the refrigerator and freezer; straighten the messiest cupboards; empty all the garbage cans in the house (even the one by the clothes dryer that's overflowing with lint); discard junk from the garage; remove all ashes from the fireplace; return anything you have borrowed; sift through your old clothes, and give away those you no longer need; balance your checkbook; pay off your bills (if you can); return all your phone calls; answer outstanding correspondence. You will be carrying on an age-old tradition of starting the new year with a clean slate.

5. Another old custom is to spend New Year's Day visiting friends. At the turn of the century, many newspapers would publish the names of those who would be "receiving" on January 1. Perhaps your paper would like to revive the custom. Or you could publish such a list in your church newsletter. If you are "receiving," it is incumbent upon you to have refreshments at the ready for your visitors.

6. Announce an open house. Ask your friends to drop by between certain hours (say, 10:00 A.M. and 6:00 P.M.) to watch the parades and

football games on television, or play games, or just visit. Suggest that they bring a covered dish to share.

7. Baby-sitting is a problem on New Year's Eve. Many people don't have the celebration they want because they can't find anyone to watch their children, much less afford it. If this is your predicament and that of your friends as well, take the initiative and offer to baby-sit for your friends' children. You might do it from, say, 6:00 New Year's Eve until 2:00 the following morning. They will pay you a modest sum for your trouble, with the understanding that one of them will do it for the following year (also for money), and so on, on a rotational basis.

8. Visit the hospital nursery on New Year's Day. Enjoy the promise of new life.

9. Wear a new shirt, scarf, or pair of slacks on New Year's Day to commemorate the new year.

10. Bury the hatchet. On New Year's Eve, write down all your disappointments, your misgivings, your hurts, your grudges, your slights. Be as specific as you need to be. Place them in an envelope, seal them, and ceremoniously toss them into the fireplace or incinerator or burn them over the kitchen sink with a vow not to carry the hurt of last year into the next.

11. Write down the things you are sorry for—your sins, in other words—and dispose of them in a similar ceremony. Ask God's forgiveness for the times you've fallen short, and for his strength to do better in the coming year. Perhaps you should also ask the forgiveness of someone you have sinned against. This is a good time to do it.

12. Make bread on New Year's Day to symbolize growth. Try something fancy—you have all day.

13. Treat yourself to a long, long-distance phone call to a friend you don't see often.

14. If you have done fall canning or freezing, delay opening the jars until January 1. Celebrate New Year's Day by tasting for the first time the foods you've put by. If you can't wait so long to dip into your stock, save out something special—the watermelon pickles, the bing cherries, or the lime marmalade—for the occasion.

15. Make a calendar on New Year's Day. Use a spiral-bound drawing tablet and felt-tipped markers for your masterpiece. Decorate each page with artwork of your own making, or that of your children, nieces, nephews, or grandchildren, or photographs from the past year. Mark special events: birthdays, anniversaries, holidays, vacations. If you aren't feeling that ambitious, get a ready-made calendar. But be sure to mark the red-letter days, using last year's calendar as a guide.

16. Plan a family celebration. Abolish bedtime rules for children (you might encourage a late-afternoon nap). Make caramel corn, spiced cider, or favorite family treats. Many foods are as fun to make as they are to eat: popcorn balls, taffy, caramel apples, roasted pumpkin seeds, decorated cookies. Talk to your children about the events of the past year, and dream about the year to come. Recall vacations, births, deaths, and milestones. Make height and weight measurements part of your New Year's Eve activities. Let children predict how tall they'll be *next* year!

The Party's Over, or A Twelfth Night Exercise

Was it better this year? Did anything improve? Did the old traditions hold up? Were your values reflected in your celebration?

On pages 8 and 9 you charted your hopes for Christmas and how past holidays had lived up to these hopes. Can you look back on that chart now and see any progress in reconciling your expectations to your values?

Perhaps just a glance down the list will answer that question. If your entire family got together for a family council planning session before Christmas, then they should have a brief time after Christmas to assess what happened.

Before Christmas, you completed these sentences:

1. "What I like most about Christmas is . . ."
2. "What I like least about Christmas is . . ."

Now finish these statements:

1. "My favorite old thing we did this year was . . ."
2. "My favorite new thing we did this year was . . ."
3. "I wish I'd had a chance to . . ."
4. "The biggest disappointment I had this year was . . ."
5. "Next year I'd like to . . ."

Sometimes even our best laid plans go awry.

"This year I decided that I wanted to make all my Christmas gifts. Which I did. In addition to costing almost as much overall as store-bought gifts would have, it took an incredible amount of time, and I ended up cutting corners at the last minute. Some of my gifts were really tacky."

"I've always wanted to go south for Christmas. This year Janet and I drove down to Miami Beach for a few days and tried to enjoy ourselves. But all along we kept thinking we should be in Boston, we should be with my mom, we should be shoveling snow. All in all, it was a pretty dismal time."

"Our family decided to cut down on what we spent for gifts. So all the brothers and sisters just drew names and we gave each other family gifts. What we realized—too late—is that aside from giving each other gifts, we don't have a lot in common. After we had opened the packages, there just wasn't anything else to do. I can see now that we relate to each other through *things*. I'm not real pleased with that, but at least I understand that now, and hopefully we can begin to make some changes."

"I was determined not to gain any more weight over the holidays. I baked for the family, but I didn't eat anything myself. I tried some low-cal holiday recipes I got from Weight Watchers, but they were pretty lame compared to turtle pie and ribbon candy. Dieting ruined the holidays for me. I thought it would be easier to diet than face the fact that I'd gained another five pounds, but I don't think so. I'd rather gain five pounds than have another Christmas like that."

When your strategies for a new, improved Christmas celebration don't work out, you could conclude that it's futile to try to change anything as written-in-granite as Christmas, or that when you try to change things you're bound to ruin everything. That's a risk. Change is nearly always a risk.

It is also nearly always a step in the right direction. Even if a plan didn't materialize as envisioned, or if a strategy was unsuccessful, or if an effort was unappreciated, it has value by virtue of the fact that for once you assessed the situation, thought of a solution, carried it out, and had hopes of improvement.

After all that has been done, don't be afraid to admit that it didn't work. You can learn, for example, that homemade gifts are not the ultimate answer to the question of how gift-giving extravagance can be brought under control; that Christmas away from home isn't what you hoped it would be; that gifts are a vital component of your family celebration; that dieting should be suspended during the holidays.

You can be assured that you have come a long way if

—you understand what your spoken and unspoken holiday expectations are,

—you can realistically assess the realities you face,

—you are willing to consider change as a method of reconciling expectations with reality.

Appendix: Resources

Greeting Cards

CURRENT
The Current Building
Colorado Springs, CO 80941

This company sells, through the mail only, an extensive line of high-quality cards, stationery, and gifts. Their pricing structure allows substantial discounts for large orders. If you can combine your order with that of your friends (encouraged by Current), you can save a bundle. Products may also be sold for fund-raising. Write for a free catalog.

ABBEY PRESS
110 Hill Drive
St. Meinrad, IN 47577

The Benedictine monks of St. Meinrad Archabbey own Abbey Press, a company that produces and sells an extensive line of Christmas and all-occasion greeting cards, religious paraphernalia of exceptional quality, and miscellaneous gifts and ornaments. Nearly all of their cards and Christmas items express Christian sentiments—increasingly hard to find in retail card shops. Their mail-order catalog is published four times a year and will be sent free of charge upon request.

Double-Duty Cards and Gifts

There are many worthwhile organizations whose work is funded in large part by the sale of cards and gifts. Most of them have reliable mail-order distribution through which you may order goods for yourself or have them sent directly to a friend or relative. All of the following will send a free catalog or brochure if requested.

KOINONIA PARTNERS
Route 2
Americus, GA 31709-9986

Koinonia Partners was founded by Clarence and Forence Jordan and Martin and Mabel England in 1942. (Clarence Jordan is the author of the Cotton Patch versions of the Gospels and Letters of the New Testament.) Their goal is to live in community and bear witness to the Christian teachings of peacemaking, loving, respect for all people, and sharing. They include among their many programs a cooperative, communal farm, literature distribution, home building for the poor in their area, a child development center for neighbors, youth missionaries, and adult education. An outgrowth of the farming and gardening is a food industry that grows pecans and peanuts.

They will gladly send your gift anywhere in the world (sometimes they charge extra for long-distance postage) and offer such delicacies as spiced pecans and peanuts, fruitcake, pecan-stuffed dates, hickory-smoked pecans, and carob-peanut crunch.

FELLOWSHIP OF RECONCILIATION
Box 271
Nyack, NY 10960

F.O.R. is an organization devoted to peacemaking around the world. In existence since 1914, it has a history of initiating and supporting efforts in justice and nonviolent resistance to war. They sell cards for the Christmas season, as well as a selection of books and pamphlets relative to their cause.

UNICEF
U.S. Committee for UNICEF—Greeting Cards
P.O. Box 5050, Grand Central Station
New York, NY 10163

UNICEF is well known for its beautiful cards and stationery. Adorned with artwork from countries around the world, these colorful and high-quality products are excellent as gifts or for your own use.

NATIONAL WILDLIFE FEDERATION
1412 16th Street, N.W.
Washington, DC 20036

The highly acclaimed *Ranger Rick* and *Your Big Backyard* magazines are available through the National Wildlife Federation, as well as an interesting assortment of books, cards, and gifts, all adorned with spectacular nature-related artwork and graphics. Members receive a 20 percent discount from the retail price of most titles.

Alternate Marketing Organizations

There has been an exciting movement in recent years among concerned churches and religious organizations to provide an outlet in this country for the native crafts of developing nations. Traditionally, artisans and craftmakers in struggling economies have produced their wares for middlemen who buy them at slave-labor prices and then make tremendous profits by marking them up substantially for resale around the world.

Several groups are now buying crafts directly from the craftmakers, paying them a fair price for their work, and selling them in this country through the mail or in their own shops, with profits plowed back into the enterprise. The result is an opportunity for local artisans to become somewhat free from exploitation and to make better wages, and for buyers in this country to enjoy foreign crafts and be challenged to think about how our own lifestyles and patterns of consumption affect other people around the world.

JUBILEE CRAFTS
300 W. Apsley Street
Philadelphia, PA 19144

A ministry of *The Other Side* magazine, Jubilee Crafts is in the business of buying crafts from Third-World markets and distributing them in the United States through their Jubilee Partners (volunteers who take it on themselves to organize selling efforts in their own communities) and direct sales through their catalogs and brochures. They carry a limited, yet eclectic, assortment of crafts, as well as some cards and books.

SELFHELP CRAFTS
240 N. Reading Road
Ephrata, PA 17522

SELFHELP Crafts is a program of the Mennonite Central Committee, a relief and service agency supported by Mennonites and Brethren in Christ. Their crafts are distributed in SELFHELP stores around the United States. With more than sixty shops, they've pretty much got the country covered. They will be glad to supply a listing of the stores, so you can see if there is one in your area.

SERRV Self-Help Handcrafts
P.O. Box 365
New Windsor, MD 21776-0365

SERRV is involved almost exclusively in selling bulk quantities of craft goods to organizations at a 20 percent discount, and then those organizations (church groups, community organizations, etc.) retail them in their community, keeping the 20 percent difference as their profit incentive. This is a worthwhile, effective way of raising money, or the money can be donated back to SERRV to continue its work. The minimum order of $50 is also well within reach for the average consumer who chooses to do some Christmas shopping via the catalog they provide.

SERRV is a program of the World Ministries Commission of the Church of the Brethren General Board, and purchases craft items from almost forty countries for its self-help program.

Bibliography &
Recommended Reading
(Denoted by *)

Barnett, James H., *The American Christmas: A Study in National Culture.* New York: Macmillan, 1954.

Baur, John E., *Christmas on the American Frontier.* Caldwell, ID: The Caston Printers, Ltd., 1961.

*Bjorn, Thyra Ferré, *Once Upon a Christmas Time.* New York: Holt, Rinehart and Winston, 1964.

Buchwald, Art, *Down the Seine and Up the Potomac with Art Buchwald.* New York: G. P. Putnam, 1977.

*Chambers, Wicke and Asher, Spring, *The Celebration Book of Great American Traditions.* New York: Harper & Row, 1983.

Cowie, L. W. and Gummer, John Selwyn, *The Christian Calendar.* Springfield, MA: G. & C. Merriam Co., 1974.

*Del Re, Gerard and Patricia, *The Christmas Almanac.* Illus. by Doug Jamieson. Garden City, NY: Doubleday, 1979.

*Dickens, Charles, *A Christmas Carol.*

Dunphy, Hubert M., *Christmas Every Christmas.* Milwaukee: The Bruce Publishing Co., 1960.

*Ehlen-Miller, Margaret, et al, *The Gift of Time: Family Celebrations and Activities for Advent, Christmas and Epiphany.* Wilton, CT: Morehouse-Barlow Company, 1977.

*Fisher, Roger and Ury, William, *Getting to Yes.* Boston: Houghton Mifflin, 1983.

Foley, Daniel J., *Christmas the World Over.* Philadelphia: Chilton, 1963.

Hartman, Rachel, *The Gifts of Christmas.* Manhasset, NY: Channel Press, 1962.

*Henry, O., "The Gift of the Magi."

Ickis, Marguerite, *The Book of Festivals and Holidays the World Over.* New York: Dodd, Mead & Co., 1970.

*Longacre, Doris Jantzen, *Living More with Less*. Scottdale, PA: Herald Press, 1980.

*Robinson, Barbara, *The Best Christmas Pageant Ever*. New York: Avon, 1972.

*Robinson, Jo and Staeheli, Jean Coppock, *Unplug the Christmas Machine: How to Have the Christmas You've Always Wanted*. New York: William Morrow, 1982.

*Robinson, Jo and Staeheli, Jean Coppock, *Unplug the Christmas Machine, Leader's Guide*, 1982.

*Sansom, William, *Christmas*. London: Weidenfeld and Nicolson, 1968.

*Shannon-Thornberry, Milo, *The Alternate Celebrations Catalog*. New York: The Pilgrim Press, 1982.

*Thomas, Dylan, *A Child's Christmas in Wales*. Illus. by Fritz Eichenberg. New York: New Directions Publishing Co., 1954.

Wilder, Laura Ingalls, *Little House in the Big Woods*. New York: Harper & Row, 1953.

———. *By the Shores of Silver Lake*. New York: Harper & Row, 1953.

———. *The Long Winter*. New York: Harper & Row, 1953.

———. *On the Banks of Plum Creek*. New York: Harper & Row, 1953.

———. *Farmer Boy*. New York: Harper & Row, 1961.

*Wilson, Dorothy, ed., *The Family Christmas Book*. Englewood Cliffs, NJ: Prentice-Hall, Inc., 1957.